SCENIC ART AND CONSTRUCTION

A PRACTICAL GUIDE

SCENIC ART AND CONSTRUCTION

Emma Troubridge and Tim Blaikie

The Crowood Press

First published in 2002 by
The Crowood Press Ltd
Ramsbury, Marlborough
Wiltshire SN8 2HR

British Library Cataloguing-in-Publication Data
A catalogue record for this book is available from the British Library.

ISBN 1 86126 499 2

Acknowledgements
Acknowledgements, and very grateful thanks to: the staff and students at RADA (from 2000 to the present); to Alasdair Flint at Flint Hire and Supply; the technical students of the Victorian College of the Arts, Melbourne; and the Royal Opera House, Carpentry Workshops. Also to: Gary Thorne, Stephen Metcalf, Niki Turner, Richard Nutbourne, Tony Nutbourne, John Smart, Dave Appleyard, Neil Fraser, Margaret O'Rourke, Alan Barnes, Barnaby Benson, Jonathan Samuels, Frances Russell, John Campbell, Frances Waddington, Christine Jones, Jim Healey, Luca Crestani, Graham Ridley, Jo McGill, Dave Woods, Mark Postlewaite, Mark Pursey and finally to C., J. and T. Healey, and J. Nelson with special love and thanks.

Grateful thanks also to the photographers: Jonathan Samuels, Richard Holtum, Mick Hurdis, Niki Turner and Jock McDougall.

Line artwork by Keith Field and Tim Blaikie.

Photograph previous page: RADA production of *Shyman at the Palace*, designed by Roger Butlin and directed by Time Caroll.

Front cover photo shows a RADA production of *Present Laughter*, by Noel Coward. Directed by Robert Chetwyn, and designed by Peter Rice.

Dedication
To all those who have inspired and supported us.

Safety is of the utmost importance in every aspect of construction work. When using tools, always follow closely the manufacturer's recommended procedures. However, the authors and publisher cannot accept responsibility for any accident or injury caused by following the advice given in this book.

Typefaces used: Cheltenham Bold Condensed (chapter headings), Photina MT (main text) and Helvetica (labels).

Typeset and designed by D & N Publishing
Baydon, Marlborough, Wiltshire.

Printed and bound in Great Britain by Antony Rowe, Chippenham.

Origination by Black Cat Graphics Ltd, Bristol, England.

CONTENTS

FOREWORD

Beyond the proscenium arch, past the stage, exists a labyrinth of workshops with inadequate space and poor facilities where the 'backstage' boys and girls work. Invariably underpaid, they devote long hours ensuring 'the show must go on'. Amongst them you will find the scenic artists and carpenters, some of whom have studied the medium and some who are self-taught, and for the artists, many are painters in their own right. Their collaborative task is to use their many skills to transform the small-scale images of the stage designer into full-scale scenery to be viewed from afar.

Each project varies enormously from a hastily drawn conception that demands an inventive interpretation to a scrupulously detailed image requiring an exacting replication. The scenic carpenter's skill lies in being able to interpret the designs and technical drawings before re-creating them into a three-dimensional practical structure. The scenic artists take over at this stage and perform their interpretative magic using a mastery of colour and texture. The process is then transformed into the desired visual setting for the drama, dance or opera to be performed.

The relationship for both scenic artist and carpenter with the designer is curious, as it is dependent on trust. The designer has to be able to let go so that the work can progress to its next stage. A successful collaboration occurs when the inherent style of the designer's creative image is adopted, as well as a sympathetic creative approach towards the design enabling the change of scale to stay fresh and thus avoiding a watered-down copy of the original.

Both artists and carpenters are capable of working in varying media, and often they excel within a preferred area. When choosing both scenic artists and carpenters for the job in hand, as much careful consideration is taken as when the director casts his actors for the performance.

Along with so many others who work in the theatre, they are unseen and therefore overlooked, apart that is by those who recognize their invaluable contribution to the theatre. They may be unsung heroes, but to me and other designers they are indeed heroic.

Maria Björnson, Theatre Designer

INTRODUCTION

For many of those who visit the theatre, the fascination derived from it is not only from the performers, but also from the visual spectacle created by stage designers. There are even fewer of us who have looked further than this and wondered in amazement at just how these creations come about. The types of questions you may ask yourselves are: How is it made? What is it is painted on? This book is intended to answer those very questions in a manner that is both practical, informative and, above all, simple. It is not intended to be the ultimate guide, as there is one way of learning far greater than this, and that is, quite simply, experience.

A book such as this hopes not only to introduce the aspiring individual to the world of backstage theatre but, more importantly perhaps, to inspire you to go out there for yourself and find out quite what a challenging, at times exhausting, but indeed fulfilling, and certainly never boring, career you may have ahead of you – whether in the field of scenic art or construction.

Starting with the basics, the book provides explanations on the production processes, advice on setting up workshops, what tools you may need, through to each and every process involved for both the scenic carpenter and artist, in bringing a stage design to a three-dimensional life-sized reality.

RADA production of **Clandestine Marriage,** *designed by Julie Nelson and directed by Peter Oyston.*

1 THE PRODUCTION PROCESSES

This chapter covers the initial viewing of the scale model, discussions with both the designer and production departments, and assessing the designer's requirements. It will also cover an introduction to estimating and budgeting for scenic construction and painting.

In order to start to build and paint a set, much needs to be done prior to cutting a piece of timber or picking up a paintbrush. As part of the production team, the members of whom all perform separate but interrelated jobs, the master carpenter and the scenic artist have several tasks to complete in what is called the pre-production period. These vary depending on the nature and scale of the production, as well as the type of company that is performing the play. At one end of the scale we have the fringe, amateur or even school production. At this level, there is not always a designer of the overall production and, indeed, the scenery is very often designed by the director, interested students or perhaps even a member of the cast. This does not preclude these productions from running in a professional manner, and many such plays manage to do so in very difficult circumstances, often facing extremely tight budgetary limitations.

For many years, the backbone of the British theatre industry was the repertory theatre system, which provided creative outlet and job opportunities for countless professionals on 'both sides of the lights'. Whilst funding cuts have seen the decline in numbers of these companies, many are still in production throughout the country. In such theatres, there would be a permanent production team whose responsibility it would be to stage each new show.

The team is made up principally of the following:

* director
* set designer
* production manager
* stage manager
* deputy stage manager
* assistant stage manager
* chief electrician
* head of sound
* prop master
* wardrobe supervisor
* scenic carpenter
* scenic artist.

When a play goes into pre-production, the director will meet with the designer to discuss the proposed visual and thematic requirements of the production. After these initial discussions, the designer will produce what is called a sketch model, which will provide a rough idea of what is intended of the production team.

The model is usually constructed at a scale of 1:25 and is, as its name suggests, a roughly finished model simply showing the basic shapes

Master Carpenter	Stage Carpenter	Assistant Carpenter
Head Painter	Scenic Artist	
Wardrobe Supervisor	Wardrobe Assistant	Dresser
Stage Manager	Deputy Stage Manager	Assistant Stage Manager
Head of Props	Prop Maker	
Chief Electrician	Stage Electrician	Lighting & Sound Operators

Creative team

Director
Designer
Lighting Designer
Sound Designer

Production Manager

(Above) Schematic diagram of production team.
(Below) A typical white card model.

and structures. This is done mainly because it is at this stage in the design process that the production team may require significant changes to the design due to structural, budgetary or legal concerns. These concerns vary from health and safety issues, such as provision of fire exits or the use of fire on stage, to the weight requirements of set pieces, specific uses of scenic elements, as well as the rough cost of a set build. Whilst the scenic carpenter and artist are not required to give exact costs of materials at this time, they are expected to be able to highlight potential costly elements.

At this stage, look out for issues that may not be shown in the model, for example:

* Are doors double- or single-sided?
* Are windows practical?
* What goes in the windows – is it acrylic, polycarbonate, gauze or nothing at all?
* Which scenic elements are load-bearing?

Because every set is different, it is difficult to highlight all possible eventualities for the scenic carpenter's attention; however, using common sense it will become clear what requires further discussion or consideration.

For the scenic artist, it is a good idea to check with the designer what are the textural and painting requirements of the set, which may have major time and budgetary implications.

Model in discussion with designer, director and production manager.

For example, are there any specific finishes such as three-dimensional brickwork, painted cloths or specialized paintwork?

The meeting provides an opportunity to iron out major concerns before too many costly decisions have been made. Usually the next time that the model is seen is at the first production meeting, when the entire team sees the design for the first time and the proposed production is discussed.

At this time, the scenic carpenter can expect to receive the technical drawings from the designer to enable him or her to begin constructing the set. The scenic artist will usually arrange a meeting with the designer for a later date to discuss in detail the required paint effects and finishes, so as to prepare samples for their approval.

QUANTIFYING AND ESTIMATING

The first practical step that the scenic carpenter and artist can take is quantifying and costing the materials required to build the set. It is vital that this is done prior to starting work because, if agreed methods of finish and construction prove to be too expensive, cheaper alternatives will have to be considered.

From a constructional perspective, now that the design has been approved, we can cost the timber requirements for flattage by square metre and linear metre. However, this only represents a fraction of the true cost of the set-build. Other cost implications include doors, door furniture such as knobs, hinges and latches, flooring requirements, handrails for stairs, skirting and architrave, as well as truck castors and brakes. All of these elements will represent a major cash outlay and must be included in any finished budget.

In scenic painting terms, once the designer has approved the samples, you are now able to estimate exactly the cost and quantities of the materials to be used. To arrive at this cost, the overall areas in square metres of the set pieces, cloths and floor surfaces will be taken into account. As well as this, the individual elements of each finish must be broken down and assessed. This will include sealers, primers, paints, textures, glazes and adhesives, as well as all fabrics such as made-up cloths. In other words, everything that it takes to get the set painted and finished to the designer's requirements.

The chart overleaf represents the budgetary breakdown for a typical box set. For this example, there are no particularly unusual requirements, and all elements of construction and painting have been included.

Using suppliers in your area, or by contacting the specialist suppliers given at the back of the book, try filling in the totals of each material to arrive at a finished budget. These contacts are invaluable for any carpenter or painter. Collecting their up-to-date price lists, catalogues, colour charts and swatches is highly recommended to build up a personal resource library.

TECH BITS ←

Costing Sheet

Production
Directors
Set & Props Designer
Production Manager

Description	Materials Required	Total units		Cost/unit	Cost/Est.	Source	Order #	Actual Cost	Delivery Date
	75mm x 25mm PAR softwood	200	m						
	50mm x 25mm PAR softwood	40	m						
	50mm x 50mm PAR softwood	40	m						
	75mm x 25mm TORUS moulding	20	m						
	150mm x 25mm TORUS moulding	30	m						
	50mm x 25mm Dado moulding	30	m						
	2440mm x 1220mm x 4mm plywood	25	shts						
	2440mm x 1220mm x 18mm plywood	10	shts						
	Shellac sealer	5	ltrs						
	Filler	1	kg						
	White emulsion paint	5	ltrs						
	Ultra Marine scenic colour	3	kg						
	Rose Madder scenic colour	1	ltr						
	25mm masking tape	4	rolls						
	Matt emulsion glaze	3	ltrs						

A typical costing sheet for a small box set.

2 THE WORKSHOP

This chapter describes how to set up and stock a carpentry workspace. Tips are given on optimal placement of heavier machinery, what tools are useful and how to lay them out for ease of access, and also, storage of timber. The chapter ends with a brief description of the fit-up: what needs to be achieved prior to the 'big day'.

Access Doors

The first task that a scenic carpenter should carry out when moving into a new workshop space is to ascertain the maximum size that it is possible to build to, whilst still being able to remove the set piece from the workshop. While this may sound obvious, it is an easy trap to fall into. Measure the diagonal opening distance of the access doors to determine the greatest width flat that can be removed from the workshop in one piece. Make a note of it for future reference.

Every workshop needs to have a dedicated area for the construction of set pieces but, due to the different demands of scenic construction, it is important to ensure that it is as flexible as possible. For work such as door and window construction, tread building and other smaller items, a traditional carpenter's bench is ideal. Usually approximately 3,000mm long by 750mm wide, it should feature a solidly constructed worktop with a trench in the middle. This trench allows easy storage of tools that are required but not in immediate use, as well as a place to put waste material prior to clearing it away and as a place for fixings and adhesives. Other features include a carpenter's vice for securing work for screwing and planing, a set of drawers for storage of tools and fixings, as well as other useful items such as jigs, bench hooks, and so on. A carpenter's bench is, by its very construction, a heavy workshop item; however, fitting wind-up castors to the underside makes it possible to move it out of the way when the floor space is needed. This will usually be necessary when a floor or cut flat is being marked out. Large treads may also require floor space and, of course, the time will come when the set has been built and it is desirable to fit it up in the workshop. in order to make sure that it goes together. All of these will require a large area of floor space and, in the case of the fit-up process, ceiling height as well. Finally, it is often preferable to construct flattage on trestles. Carpenter's trestles are an invaluable element of any workshop, providing flexible support for the construction or painting of many scenic elements. Flats, by their very nature, are best constructed on trestles, as they can be moved easily to necessary points of support, whilst allowing easy access to all areas of the work piece. Equally importantly, they fold away neatly, taking up little space when not in use. A set of eight wooden trestles will be very useful in any workshop.

WORKSPACE

When looking for suitable workshop space, a good rule is to think of the maximum height that sets will be built to (this will vary depending on the size of the theatre). Allow an extra 300mm in ceiling height for clearance. The building of a set is made much easier if it is possible to stand set pieces up prior to taking them into the theatre. This will allow for the fitting of mouldings and so on, as well as the time-saving process of ironing out any fitting problems in the workshop rather than in the theatre. As well as ceiling height, every workshop needs plenty of floor space: wood machines are bulky things that take up a lot of space and constructing and then storing the scenery also takes up space.

The last critical consideration when choosing a workshop is the 'get in': how easy will it be to get materials and scenery in and out of the workshop itself? The ideal workshop should be located very close to the painter's studios, as well as close to the theatre. Most important, however, is the size of the access. Scenery can come in all shapes and sizes, and a large workshop space is made less efficient by having a small doorway. A roller door is ideal, allowing for long, thin flattage, as well as bulky trucks and tread sets. A loading bay providing access for lorries is also highly desirable.

Machine Placement

Do not forget when placing machines in position to allow for room around the machines for the timber itself. For example, a radial-arm saw will need at least 4,000mm on each side of the blade and a tilt arbor saw needs to have the size of a sheet of 2,440 × 1,220mm material all around the blade. Without these considerations, the tools will be next to useless.

HAND TOOLS

Look in any experienced carpenter's tool bag and you will see all sorts of weird and wonderful tools that have been collected over the years. For the novice, however, many of these tools will prove to be an unnecessary expense when funds are tight. A useful list will rate each hand tool in order of importance, with the higher number of stars indicating greater need but not excluding the occasional vital tool. The tools listed below will be invaluable in the construction of even the most basic of sets.

Essential Hand Tools ***
Claw hammer, panel saw, tenon saw, tape measure (minimum of 5m but ideally 8m), 1m folding ruler, set of chisels (6mm, 10mm, 12mm, 18mm, 25mm, 38mm), combination square, block plane, Pozidriv 2 screwdriver, slotted screwdriver, drill and drill bits (1.5–12.5mm), countersink bit.

Useful Tools **
Roofing square, smoothing plane, Yankee screwdriver, nail punch, pincers, trimming knife, spirit-level, chalk line.

Occasional Tools *
Adjustable bevel, mallet (these days, plastic-handled chisels are more than capable of withstanding the blows of a hammer but mallets are vital when using wooden-handled chisels), 2 × speed clamps, adjustable wrench, coping saw.

POWER TOOLS

Over the past 20 years, scenic construction has become more efficient and cost-effective through the advent of reasonably priced, high-quality power tools. These machines have quickly replaced many well-loved, manual equivalents. It is rare to see a carpenter using a coping saw these days, when an electric jigsaw

(Above) The vital tools of the trade.
(Below) Some useful additions.

These will come in handy from time to time.

Tools: General Care and Storage

For the genuine enthusiast, it is worth spending a little bit extra on tools to get better quality products. It will save time in the future, avoiding expensive set corrections due to inaccurate or substandard equipment; they will also prove to be more durable, as well as holding a sharp edge for longer. Remember though, as the stars denote, start by buying the basics and get the rest as you need them. If the bulk of the carpenter's time is to be spent in the workshop itself, it may be preferable to construct a shadow board on which to store the hand tools. At a glance it is possible to locate the desired tool, as well as see if any tools are missing. To make a simple shadow board, simply lay the tool collection out in an ordered fashion on a sheet of 18mm ply, and by use of nails, hooks and clips, devise methods of holding the tools on the board. Once the board has been mounted on the wall, draw around the outside of each tool with a thick black marker and fill in the silhouette with black paint, hence forming a 'shadow' effect.

will do the job quicker and better. Similarly, the carpenter's brace has been almost completely superseded by the power drill and cordless screwdriver. The cordless screwdriver is an extremely useful tool that has revolutionized scenic construction in the past 10 years. It has made the construction of scenery, as well as the fitting-up of sets in the theatre, much more economical in relation to time constraints, and has become almost overnight the first tool of choice when starting out in the scenic-construction industry. When investing in a cordless screwdriver, it is a good idea to ensure that it has a minimum of 9.6 volts and comes with a spare battery. This will ensure that, as well as doing the job, it will also always be charged and ready for action. Many 'bargains' only come with one battery, therefore imposing a mandatory down-time while it is recharging. Ideally, the screwdriver should be between 12 and 14 volts as this will provide optimum performance due to increased power and torque; however, as with every other area of scenic construction, it is necessary to cut the cloth to suit the purse.

The next tool that should be added to the kit is a jigsaw. This tool is enormously versatile and, indeed, can sometimes be overused in

Exercise

An excellent exercise in basic scenic joinery, as well as providing a useful tool, is to construct a set of trestles. Working from the supplied technical drawing and the information in Chapters 4 and 5, try constructing a set of trestles from 25 × 75mm PAR softwood. A well-built set will last for many years and be in almost constant use.

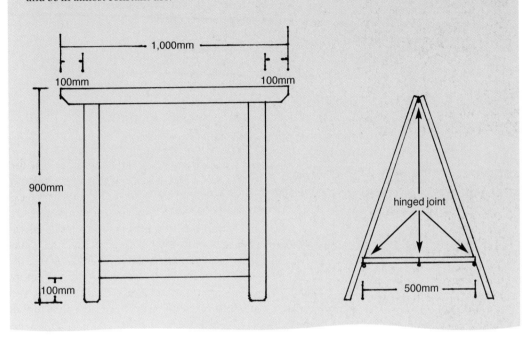

(Above) Technical drawing of workshop trestle.

A jigsaw can be used for cutting the tightest of curves.

Cutting with a Jigsaw

When using a jigsaw for delicate plywood cutting, always ensure that the jigsaw is set to zero intensity, as this will prevent break-out and splintering of the grain. It is worth looking at the blade-changing mechanism on the model that you are choosing. These days, certain patented methods will make the process very quick and simple.

inexperienced hands. In scenic construction, however, it is used for cutting plywood and light softwoods. The variety of blades available make this tool tremendously useful for cutting metals, both ferrous and non-ferrous, plastics and a variety of specialist sheet materials. When choosing a jigsaw, it is advisable to pick one with variable speed, as well as intensity. The intensity usually is available in four settings and makes ripping softwood and rough-cutting quicker and more effective.

The power drill is a tool that many people feel can be replaced by the cordless screwdriver. However, if optimum output is required from the tools, then consider investing in a good quality drill. The cordless screwdriver is more than adequate for drilling holes up to 6.5mm in diameter; however, holes in excess of this will cause undue stress on the motor. As well as this, it drains the battery of valuable power, which takes time to recharge. The power drill is particularly useful for drilling into metal and masonry, as with its increased voltage, it makes drilling into these substances much more efficient. The drill of choice should ideally have a 12mm keyless chuck, which will save time in operation, as well as avoiding the problem of losing the chuck key – a most common and really rather annoying occurrence! It should have variable speed, as well as forward and reverse. Finally, wherever possible, try to get a drill with a masonry setting. This will prove useful when fitting-up in the theatre, primarily when working in a studio environment.

Having acquired screwing and drilling tools, as well as a tool that will cut the irregular shapes of any designer's whim, the next step is to look at investing in a good-quality circular saw. This tool will prove invaluable in a small workshop, particularly one that does not have the benefit of a tilt arbor, radial arm or wall saw. The hand-

The power drill has replaced all hand drills. Try to get one with forward and reverse.

The circular saw in use with a ripping fence.

held circular saw is capable of cutting sheet materials to parallel widths, softwood to length, as well as most other cutting tasks in the scenic-construction field. It is useful for rebating, housing and ripping, and used properly is an invaluable tool for the scenic carpenter. The circular saw usually comes with a fence for ripping; however, the author has found that the most effective method of repetitive straight ripping can be achieved by using a very simple jig, which can be applied in many ways and to many tools.

The fence provides the user with a straight, consistent edge to cut to and also, being set to the width of the outer edge of the circular saw's base plate, makes marking-out very simple.

When marking-out without the fence, it is necessary to mark twice: once for the position of the saw cut and once for the position of the straight edge; whereas with the fence, only one mark is necessary. The last vital hand tool, and sadly the most expensive, is the router. This most versatile of tools is capable of both decorative and structural tasks. The router can give the edge of a table an antique or period style, as well as trimming an overhang on the edge of a flat. It will also create realistic planking effects in a sheet of ply (a similar fence set-up to the circular saw fence can be easily applied), as well as cut a perfect circle or arch.

The router with a variety of bits.

It is recommended that a medium to high wattage (i.e. no less than 1,100W) router is used; however, as usual, always aim to keep within budget. A suitable dust-extraction system built into the unit is also highly desirable for both health and safety, and housekeeping reasons.

The End Stop

Mass production of set pieces such as flats or rostra can lead to tedious, repetitive work. An end stop can be used when carrying out these tasks, removing the need to measure each individual length of timber. Ensure that the stop has an allowance for the collection of dust, which will ensure neat and accurate work and save valuable time.

An end stop in position. Note the notch at the bottom to help prevent dust build-up.

With a little practice, this tool will prove invaluable to the scenic carpenter; however, it is important to point out that the router is only as good as the router bits used in it. To this end, it is important to use tungsten carbide bits: they will maintain their edge for longer and give a vastly superior finish to regular steel bits. Although they are more expensive, they are worth it in the long run.

That covers the basic hand-held power tools that the scenic carpenter requires. However, with a little extra budget, the workshop can be made even more efficient. Wood machines come in a range of qualities from the most basic handyman tool to the most sophisticated of industrial machines. The thing that will decide which to buy is very simple: how much can you afford? For the beginner, the above-mentioned tools will suffice but for the carpenter looking to produce a high-quality product, there are a few tools that could be invested in.

The radial-arm saw is the most useful of wood machines. With the ability to cross-cut (cut across the grain), rip (cut along the grain), bevel (cut the timber to an angle) and trench (cut less than the full depth of the timber), this tool is invaluable in any workshop. Without doubt, the radial-arm saw's best application is cross-cutting, which is particularly useful when building flats or floors. The other features of the saw are useful when no other tool is available but should be seen more as a 'make do' rather than the ideal.

Other tools recommended, depending on available funds, are a band saw, rip saw and mortiser and tenoner. All of these will dramatically change the efficiency of the running of the workshop, as well as improving construction quality. It is up to the individual to gauge the need for such tools, depending on the workload expected to be encountered.

Use the guidance given in this book to help you to decide whether it is worth the financial outlay, as it may be preferable to do this a bit at a time.

TIMBER STORAGE

Before the timber order arrives, it is necessary to plan ahead and create workshop space for the timber. Remember, it can take up a lot of space, so look into the potential for wall-mounted racking: it gets the timber off the floor out of harm's way and leaves the workshop clear of clutter. In addition to this, it is the best way to store timber, providing good all-round airflow, as well as making stock-taking easier.

When deciding on a suitable location for storage racking, take into account the following points:

* try to make it easy to offload from the lorry;
* try to locate it near the radial-arm saw.

The radial-arm saw is used first when constructing a flat, so avoid double-handling by having the timber near by.

A similar rack is useful for the storage of sheet material. Standard sheet sizes tend to be 2,440 × 1,220mm, so either a flat rack or a horizontally stacked rack will be very useful to divide up the different sorts of materials. Ply-

wood (4mm, 6mm, 12mm and 18mm), as well as hardboard and other specialist materials such as flexi-ply, are all used on a regular basis and should all be kept in stock.

Once the timber has arrived, sort it into length, thickness and width, to assess the order and nature of it. Ideally, the softwood lengths that you ordered have been sent, but do not count on it – the timber yard deals in linear metres and will send the nearest possible lengths. This may mean an adjustment to construction plans, for example the timber may

Timber storage need not take up a great deal of space.

need to be joined in order to achieve the desired length. Sheet materials are far easier to sort and store. As they are quite heavy, it is a good idea to have their storage point as close to the entrance as possible.

Finally, every well-equipped workshop should have a set place for the storage of fixings and adhesives. A set of wall-mounted boxes is ideal. Try to locate the boxes near to the main construction area, thereby reducing the need to travel long distances. Keeping the fixings stock in full view makes for easy stock-taking, allowing the carpenter to top up any low stocks at a glance.

With the workshop laid out with tools in their right place, timber and fixings stored safely and efficiently, as well as provision for plenty of workspace, the workshop is now ready for production.

THE FIT-UP

At this stage, it is perhaps appropriate to look at the end result of the hard work put in to reproducing the designer's concept. This book will deal mainly with the time spent in the workshop building the actual set, however the time spent in the theatre can be greatly enhanced by following a few pointers. Refer back to this section when you feel it is appropriate. Get-in, fit-up, bump-in, load-in or technical week are all terms that refer to the day, week or even month set aside to put all the hard work done in the workshop and paint studio into the theatre. Constructing the set in its final resting-place can be an extremely stressful time for all concerned, but with careful planning and preparation the process can be made productive and even pleasurable! The following account touches briefly on what must be achieved prior to the big day or, as it is referred to here, the 'fit-up'. Much of what is suggested may appear obvious, however it is surprising how the simple things can make an enormous difference.

Put the Set Together in Advance!

The flats have been built and painted, doors have had their mouldings added, rostra and treads have been constructed. It is surprising though how many sets do not get put together prior to the fit-up. Often this is due to height restrictions within the workshop environment but it is highly recommended to make every effort to do so. When more than one person is working on a build, it is not unusual for small discrepancies to creep into the various set components, leaving a potential headache for fit-up time. The critical points to check off the list are as follows:

* Fit all flattage together: use pin hinges as a means of fixing together, they allow for easy disassembly and re-assembly in the theatre. Allow one hinge approximately every 1,000mm.
* Hang all doors and fit door furniture such as handles, knockers and bells, letterboxes, latches and closers. Use lift-off hinges for the hanging of doors, as they allow for easy removal for transport; they also make for quick changes if multiple doors are needed during the run of a play.
* Fit handrails and balustrades to all treads. Ensure that intersecting handrails fit and are easily re-attached.
* Fit all cornices and skirtings. These components can contribute to creating a solid appearance to both the top and bottom of the set but they do involve care in cutting and fitting. Use a mitre cutter to cut all external corners and scribe all internal corners.
* Fit French and stage braces to the rear of the set, using pin hinges and screw eyes, as necessary.

With the set assembled, label the flats and other set components on their backs. As a rule the following information should be included:

* production name, e.g. *The Summer of the Seventeenth Doll*;

* flat position, e.g. DSR;
* flat type and number, e.g. door flat 3.

When a painted floor is being used, label the individual components in the same way but include an arrow indicating down-stage. This will aid in the installation at fit-up time. Mark the boards out on a ground plan and keep in the site box along with all other technical drawings and a scale rule.

The Site Box

A box containing all the necessary tools is vital for all fit-ups. Make a list of all hand and power tools needed, as well as all necessary ironmongery and fixings including screws, bolts, nails, glue and so on. Always err on the generous side, as it is unacceptable to have to make a dash to the hardware in the middle of a busy fit-up, where time is of the essence. To effectively do this, work through the fit-up process on paper, referring to technical drawings and the model box.

The first task in any fit-up is to do a mark-up on the stage, so for this include the ground plan, scale rule, chalk line, long tape measure and PVC tape.

Laying the floor will require either nails or narrow-mouth staples, so hammers and staplers will be required. Also, if you are using staples, you will need an air compressor and air lines.

After these specialized areas, general tools will suffice. However, the critical tools to remember are as follows:

* cordless screwdrivers
* adjustable wrenches
* hammers

The Golden Rules

- Keep safe; always use correct personal protection equipment for the job.
- Plan ahead; you can never be too organized! Filing/card systems, building schedules, fit-up schedules and crew lists all contribute to an efficient build process.
- Communicate with all relevant departments and colleagues. Keep them informed of what you are doing and what you want them to be doing.
- Strive for accuracy. Small inaccuracies throughout a build can result in unsightly joints, unsafe treads and generally shoddy finish.

* jigsaws
* hand saws
* power drill and spare drill bits
* extension leads.

Note that the above list will always need to be added to, depending on the size and nature of the set; but it is a start. With the get-in day approaching, it is time to finally finish the job started several weeks earlier. With careful planning and teamwork, it should be done efficiently and within the prescribed deadlines. Once the set has been fitted up, all that is left for the scenic carpenter to do is replenish stock levels, tidy the workshop and await any maintenance work that arises from the rigours of the performance process. Take this moment to enjoy a job well done and perhaps reflect on some of the points that have made this a successful process.

3 THE SCENIC PAINTSHOP

In this chapter the layouts and components that go into making up a scenic paintshop will be detailed. An explanation is given of the necessary tools that are needed in order to operate efficiently, as well as a list of the basic tools a beginner should acquire to get started. The maintenance of all tools is also highlighted. Spatial layout and basic workshop organization will be taken into account, covering storage of materials as well as relevant COSHH (Control of Substances Hazardous to Health) regulations and health and safety considerations.

INTRODUCTION

Now we shall look at a typical scenic paintshop and describe a workspace where a more substantial budget is available, in order to give the reader an idea of what to expect from major theatres, independent scenic studios, or indeed theatre educational establishments. Obviously this is not possible for the amateur or an individual setting out on their own, where there will be many more limitations, not at least a financial one. However, there will be a lot of similarities and it is important to have a look at these. A lot can be achieved in lesser circumstances with sound common sense and good organization. At some time or other in their careers, most scenic artists will have experienced painting entire sets in the most obscure places, such as corridors, disused sheds and even backyards, weather permitting! Ideally, the scenic paintshop and the carpentry workshop are situated next to each other, with the obvious practical reason of moving scenery from one workshop to another, as well as good accessibility for the many interrelated discussions, observations and, indeed, any preparatory work that can be done in advance by the painters, whilst scenery is still in the construction process.

A Word about 'Prep' Work

The scenic artists are usually the last to start work on the set, in order of production. Consequently, in a job where time schedules are nearly always tight, it is always good to get on with any work in advance, such as preparation work. Preparation work, such as filling and sanding of constructed wooden scenery, prior to commencing the artwork, is a job often shared by both painters and carpenters alike, at both amateur and professional levels. It is a very important process that, when done well, is a major contributor to the final professional finish. It is also extremely beneficial if some of this work can be done in the carpenter's workshop, in order to keep the painting area as dust-free as possible. But remember to respect each other's space, to return any borrowed tools, to clear up afterwards and to wear the appropriate protective clothing or equipment. Above all, maintaining a good relationship with each other is important in a profession that demands successful teamwork. Other examples of useful 'prep' work include scaling up the model pieces, sampling and mixing colours, all of which will be discussed in greater detail later in the book.

(Right) Typical scenic paint-shop for floor painting.

(Below) Paint frame with gantry.

The Workspace

A scenic paintshop is ideally a large, smooth, wooden-floored space devoid of any obstructions such as pillars or low ceilings. A good approximate size to accommodate an average smaller theatre set would be from about 150m^2. As with the carpentry workshop, excellent access is vital, as well as a correct ceiling height, which must exceed the highest piece of scenery when standing up. This will almost always need to be the case prior to the fit-up on stage, either to be looked at by the designer or to allow frequent movement in and round the workshops, as well as to be worked on by various people, such as metalworkers, carpenters or scenic artists.

Within a theatre, workshops are ideally situated as close to the stage as possible. This makes the transportation of the set that much quicker and easier for the fit-up. Closer to technical week, time is always limited, with tight schedules for the many departments involved. Work will very often continue on a set once it is fitted up on stage and there will be plenty of equipment to transport for this purpose, such as paints, tools and such like. For this reason alone, there should not be a great distance between the two. In a completely independent workshop situated away from the theatre, as is often the case, work continued on stage is called a *paintcall*. Here a number of hours, or perhaps occasionally days, is specifically set aside for painting work to be done. It can often be overnight, as a production may be in full rehearsal or run. An organized touch-up box with essentials is prepared and this will be described in further detail later in this chapter.

Lighting and Electrics

Lighting and electrics in the workspace are extremely important. Preferably some natural light is required for colour matching and mixing, yet too much direct natural light can be disadvantageous, as bright sunlight or cloud movement creates confusing shadows as images shift and tones change over such large surfaces. It is therefore important to try and keep the lighting as even and bright as possible. A lot of work may be done in evenings or at night, where artificial lighting will automatically be used in the form of tungsten, halogen or daylight-simulation bulbs. Wherever possible, try to use the daylight hours to do any work requiring natural light, such as mixing colour when referring to a model or colour reference. This can prove to be really useful, as a near perfect colour match will often be required and can be difficult to achieve under the wrong lighting, with the result that expensive mistakes are made.

For electrics, it is obviously important to have a good number of power points and, where often scenery will be stacked up against the walls, a system of power points suspended from the ceiling is ideal. These need to be measured at a correct height to enable the painter to plug in, as well as be clear of heads of people walking and working underneath! A number of extension leads is also invaluable, but it is important that they are situated in a safe and non-obstructive manner.

Heating and Ventilation

Heating a paintshop is another important matter. Apart from keeping a pleasant temperature for the workers, there is often a lot of material that needs to be dried more rapidly in order to get the scenery finished, and an extra boost of heating is occasionally required. The most widely used is that of a system of fan heaters, which can rapidly heat up a space, as well as cool down, when required. In a less well-equipped studio, heaters can always be hired for a specific job, and is a far less costly method. In the middle of winter this is an absolute necessity. Some workshops are situated in far from ideal buildings and sometimes a space will have been hired for a specific job. In this situation, the size available may well have been the main consideration, in order to accommodate the set for painting, and consequently the hiring in of extra heating is imperative. Most local plant hire firms supply these at a cost that will be far less than that incurred by the delay if paint or textures are not dry in time. An important final point on this subject is appropriate ventilation. Most well-equipped paintshops will have an excellent system of ventilation and extractor fans already installed, but where there is not, it is vital that this is taken into account when working with potentially hazardous materials, such as certain glues and paints, as well as simply creating a pleasant and healthy work environment. Extractor fans are also available for hire at your local hire shop.

The Sink Area

As light and heating are two significant factors within the workspace, so indeed is a constant supply of water. A large sink with excellent drainage, in the form of extra-wide plug holes, is vital. Both hot and cold water are needed, and plenty of it. This is not only for mixing up large quantities of paint and textures, but also for the all-important cleaning-

up processes too. A good, regular supply of clean brushes and buckets in a wide variety of sizes is required. It is a known fact that most scenic sinks will, at some time or another, get blocked up due to the regular cleaning-out of old paint in buckets, as well as brushes. To reduce this happening so often, it is advisable to keep an old bucket handy to pour in any old thick paint or texture. Keep a sieve over the main plug hole: this can be made out of a stainless steel, fine-metal mesh, and bent and cut into position, and will fit any sized sink. Cleaning out a blocked U-bend is not on the scenic job description, yet it somehow sneaks into most painter's experience, and is not one of the most enjoyable.

A good supply of shelves around the sink area, preferably made up of wire mesh or open wooden slats, is important for the drainage and storage of recently washed buckets and paint trays. A system for hanging up wet brushes, rollers and other necessary cleaning equipment, such as scrubbing brushes, scrapers, and bottle brushes is also required. For brushes, drilling small holes through the handles, if they do not already have them, and hanging them on neatly spaced, filed-down nails is a

The sink area with mixing table.

very efficient method. This ensures that the water drains out the right way, and does not collect in the ferrule and destroy the bristles. Sponge rollers can be similarly stored by hanging them over a rack or pole to ensure that the foam can dry clear of any obstruction. When dried in contact with other items, distortion may occur and makes the roller useless.

Under the sink, or at least nearby, there should be a constant supply of cleaning fluids, such as a gentle detergent for cleaning brushes, particle soaps, gels and barrier creams for hands. Stronger cleaners, such as bleaches, white spirit, gun cleaners or methylated spirits, are needed at times and should always be kept in a separate lockable metal cupboard. This is an important health and safety issue, which is discussed further later in this chapter.

Paint Storage

Many scenic paintshops have a separate room for storing stock paints. In the larger studios, where a large supply is constantly needed, this room is kept under lock and key, and in order to meet budget requirements, there are regular stock checks. It is a good idea to make this stock-check list easily accessible in the paintshop as a way of quickly checking up on any stock without the need to hunt the shelves. Another useful tip is to keep a regular supply of the most frequently used materials, such as black and white emulsions or polythene. For quick and easy identification have a system of written labels to differentiate between the colours and different manufacturers. Another method is to identify the colours with corresponding coloured labels. Tightly lidded containers are needed for pigments, and these should be well labelled to state their colours. Handy stackable storage units are an efficient way of organizing the large amount of equipment needed for the scenic paintshop.

Plenty of shelving, containers and wall racks or rolling systems are needed for items such as rolls of polythene, brown paper, drawing materials, scenic fabrics and PPE (personal protective equipment). Certain textures, for example brands like Idenden or sacks of Artex, are both messy to store and mix, and are covered by a number of health and safety regulations. Professional paintshops are often equipped with a separate room designated for this, but, where this is not possible, an area cordoned-off by polythene on the floor is sufficient only if all appropriate health and safety practices are followed, such as wearing the correct ventilator masks and gloves. Under health and safety guidelines, certain paints and materials

Paint and storage shelving.

Storage units and handy labelling.

need to be stored in lockable metal cupboards. These include aniline dyes, French enamel varnishes, spirit-based stainers, solvents, thinners, strippers, oil-based paints and varnishes, and any substance that is known to be potentially hazardous. It is now common practice in scenic art to use fewer toxic materials, as potential hazards caused by these materials are now more clearly recognized. In a response to this, most manufacturers of specialist scenic materials are producing non-toxic alternatives for many products. However, whilst there are still hazardous substances in use, it is always worth checking all the relevant COSHH information and keep them safely stored. (A description of COSHH is given further in this chapter.)

The final items that need to be stored are *show colours.* Paint that is not used up in the process of painting a set is kept for valuable 'touch-ups', for use during the run of a show. (It is wise to separate these into smaller buckets, cover them and clearly mark them, e.g. Romeo and Juliet: balcony stone colour, floor glaze, act one prime.) It is then important to keep these until the very end of the show, as they are vital. If they are clearly marked, it makes the job for the stage-management team, and yourselves, a lot easier.

THE PAINT-MIXING AREA

The mixing of colour is both a vital and, at times, highly enjoyable task for the scenic artist. The mixing of both large and small quantities of prime, paint and textures is needed primarily for sampling, as well as for painting the actual set. (For sampling, *see* Chapter 10.) It is important to designate an area for this process, with a large table placed in a position of excellent light and situated, preferably, near the sink. The table surface will eventually resemble a colourful moon landscape. It is a good idea to have a smaller, yet full range, of scenic paint colours on shelves nearby from which to mix, and only use the larger stocks when needed. For mixing paint and textures, a good supply of mixing sticks, plungers, cheap brushes and, ideally, a paint-mixing drill, are also required. (An illustration of a plunger is given in Chapter 15.)

Paint manufacturers supply a wide variety of colour charts. These are an excellent visual guide to fix to the walls around the paint-mixing table. A designer may refer to certain colours whilst in discussion with the painter, and a quick glance at these charts can aid decision-making.

THE DRAWING TABLE

In a scenic paintshop there will be a certain amount of work that needs to be done in a clean and dry environment, such as looking at technical drawings, and scaling-up the model. If there is not a separate room available, it is advisable to have an area designated solely to this, with a flat table (a foldaway one is particularly useful for smaller workshops) and a good blackboard on the wall nearby for the many scribbles and calculations. A blackboard can be easily made out of an old piece of wood, sanded, primed and painted in a couple of coats of blackboard paint.

WALL SPACE

The walls of the paintshop are also a useful way of utilizing the entire space, as well as the floor. Apart from using the walls to store the scenery during the various processes of work until completion, a wooden frame is often built onto a wall in order to paint smaller canvasses, if an actual paint frame is not present. The floor of the studio will so often be filled up with either the built scenery, or cloths tacked out onto it, so any extra space is extremely useful. The frame can be made to the full height of the wall, as ladders can be used to paint the cloths if too high to reach when standing.

TOOLS

The definition of 'tool' in the dictionary describes its scenic art purpose perfectly, which is: anything used as a means of achieving an end. A scenic artist's tool collection is as versatile and varied as the image that it is helping to re-create. Where a painter decorator, car mechanic or dentist has a collection of *specific* tools for their trade, in scenic art the diversity of images that need to be created call for a far wider and more eclectic collection. More often than not, where a specific effect is required, a tool will be invented at the time. In this section we will look at the necessary basics tools needed for:

* the scenic paintshop;
* the scenic artist's personal toolbox;
* the 'touch-up box' for use in theatre.

Other curious devices used in the scenic trade will be listed, and an explanation of their uses given in their appropriate chapters.

Clean area designated to looking at technical drawings, scaling-up the model and so on.

List of Essential Basic Tools and Equipment for a Scenic Paintshop

- A-frame ladders (preferably a selection of sizes).
- Claw hammers.
- Clouts/nails/staple guns/staples/staple remover.
- Handsaw.
- Metre ruler.
- Cloth tape measure (preferably 30m).
- Pair of pliers.
- Straight edges (for a description, *see* Chapter 12).
- Spirit-level.
- Plumb-line.
- Chalk line/chalks/charcoal/drawing sticks.
- Flogger.
- Extension leads.
- Roofing square.
- Scissors.
- Stanley knife.
- Paint-mixing drill/heat gun/hairdryer.
- Set of filling knives.
- Set of trestles (details of how to make these are given in Chapter 2).

This list gives the basic essentials, but where there is a bigger budget, here is a list of tools that would be an excellent investment:

- Set of drawing tools, to include: set squares (45/90 degree and 30/60 degree), protractor and compass.
- Trammel heads.
- Compressor/air gun (these can be hired on a daily basis); air texture gun.
- Scaffold paint bridge (a device used for observing work done on the floor from a height, which enables designer and painter to look, and discuss, the work together, rather than one at a time from an A-frame ladder).

Many of the tools can be hung on shadow boards (as described in Chapter 2) for easy identification but, perhaps more importantly, as a way of ensuring their safe return! It is a far easier way of seeing exactly what is missing. Nailing out cloths requires a lot of nails, and the easiest way to store them is in open boxes with handles, so that they can be carried around – the hammer can sit inside whilst in transit too. For those who prefer to use staple guns, open boxes can be used for storing the spare staple boxes. If a variety of sizes is required, keep them in a separate box clearly marked for quick identification, for example 4mm, 3mm, 5mm, and so on.

SCENIC PAINTER'S TOOLBOX

With the diversity of skills needed to be a scenic artist, a personal set of tools is required, close at hand at all times. This toolbox is as important as the musical instrument that a musician plays on. Whether you are working full-time in a paintshop or freelancing from pillar to post, you will constantly require many items. Do not be tempted to rely on other painters, or indeed studios, as this can never be reliable. The toolbox is not the same as a paintbrush bag, which is a separate item, and will be listed in the chapter on painting.

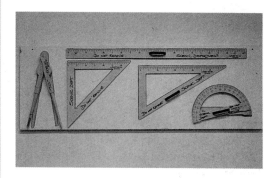

A typical shadow board.

Toolbox Contents

- Scale rule to include 1:25.
- Handsaw.
- Claw hammer.
- Staple gun and spare staples.
- Staple remover.
- Adjustable spanner.
- Tape measure (30m is the largest available, and will cover practically all your requirements; anything smaller and time can be wasted and mistakes made when working on large scenery and cloths).
- Spirit-level.
- Plumb-line.
- Selection of white and coloured chalks and charcoals.
- Chalk line.
- Set of filling knives.
- Window scraper (this is really useful for doing your prep work, filling, etc.).
- Piece of sandpaper (also useful for prep work).
- Stanley knife and spare blades.

- Collection of pencils, marker pens, chinagraph pencils, and a thin drawing pen.
- Roll of masking tape.
- Pair of scissors.
- An old screwdriver (this is for opening tins of paint).
- Artist's diffuser (this is a really handy tool for touch-ups on stage or 'breaking down' props and bits of a set).
- Pair of pliers (these are really useful for removing any old staples left in frames, or other nails, etc., that may need removing).
- A calculator (this is optional for those who do not trust their mental arithmetic skills!).
- A spray-gun (this is optional as it is an expensive item; eventually, if the genuine enthusiast wishes to continue in this field, this would be a wise investment as it should last you a whole career if well maintained).

The box itself should be as lightweight as possible, preferably with a removable tray inside, and large enough to house the tools required, but not so big that it cannot be carried comfortably. Certain items may be added or removed, depending on the requirements of a particular job, so it is important to have a good size. Such toolboxes are readily available from most builder's merchants and DIY stores, and are not too expensive.

TOUCH-UP BOX

A touch-up box contains all the necessary equipment and materials for use on stage during any paintcalls or subsequent set maintenance. It should be organized in such a way that whoever is sent to work on a set, they should be able to fully complete the work in hand without the need to regularly transport tools and materials to the appropriate venue. The box should contain the following:

* all relevant show colours and or textures, labelled clearly;
* polythene sheeting (you will often need to work in clean spaces and on existing pieces of scenery, it is therefore extremely important that this is used both to protect and as a masking);
* the appropriate tools/brushes/rollers, etc., that have been used in that particular production;
* a 'scenic' first-aid kit: scissors, glues, rags, hairdryer or heat gun, glue gun, masking tape, gaffer tape;
* buckets;
* an extension lead;
* extension handles;
* torch (with batteries).

HEALTH AND SAFETY ISSUES

Before anyone reads this section, it is worth thinking about exactly what health and safety is really concerned with. A list of legal regulations and facts on such issues will seem a thousand miles from the reality of day-to-day working experience, but accidents can and all too often do occur. Never assume that it will never happen to you, as it could be as simple as a deep wound inflicted by a simple misuse of a sharp tool or, more subtly, a devastating illness created over many years of misuse of a certain toxic material. Ignorance is probably your most dangerous enemy in this respect.

Any one considering working in technical theatre has an obligation to acquaint themselves with the rules and regulations that concern health and safety matters. Up until 1974, when the Health and Safety at Work Act was passed, these issues had not been considered important enough, yet statistically it was seen that 60 per cent of all accidents and ill health were due to management and administrative failings. Consider the work that is done in both scenic art, as well as construction, and one can get an idea of quite how potentially hazardous it can be. Here is a list of potential dangers:

* the use of ladders, tallescopes, scaffolding paint bridges, tall scenery and so on;
* the use of heavy fixed machinery, as well as powered hand tools;
* the use of materials containing toxic elements;
* the use of flammable liquids;
* working in potentially old and unsafe buildings, rented workspaces and so on.

The last example could highlight a number of different health and safety issues alone, such as the use of leaded paint, a risk of asbestos, poor maintenance of electrics, an absence of the correct kind of fire extinguishers or escapes, poor ventilation, unhygienic washing facilities, and an absence of any form of first aid. All these show us quite how, in the ever-increasing world of freelancing and self-employment, it is vital that we make ourselves aware of exactly what can be done to reduce these risks. Under government guidelines, compulsory regulations have been set up to help ensure a better working environment. More recently, these have become the responsibility of both the employer as well as the employee, in any workplace. A list is given below of a number of relevant regulations. These require that a risk assessment is undertaken by all responsible parties; there are variations in the requirements of each of those listed. Those responsible for work environments have a legal responsibility to make all information available by keeping the details of appropriate regulations on file, as well making them visible via a number of display posters around the workplaces. Here is a list of some of the appropriate regulations with which readers will need to acquaint themselves:

* Control Of Substances Hazardous to Health (COSHH) (1999): this ensures that all manufacturers supply a detailed data sheet containing all the relevant information about any materials sold;
* Manual Handling Operations Regulations (1992);
* Personal Protective Equipment At Work Regulations (PPE) (1992);
* Lead Regulations (1998);
* Asbestos Regulations (1987);
* Noise Regulations (1989);
* Management Regulations (1992);
* Fire Precautions Regulations (1997).

It is important that anyone who wishes to know more about these should obtain the correct details either from an employer or directly from institutions such as the Health and Safety Executive, details of which are listed at the end of the book.

Finally, there will always be a hefty accumulation of rubbish in the paintshop – especially when working on a textured set and using materials such as foam rubber, polystyrene, or micafil. If the paintshop is left to get too messy, it will become a potential health and safety issue, and is basically dangerous. Therefore, a regular sweep-up and general tidy is important. This requires a number of industrial brooms, dustpan and brushes, and dustbins. The brooms and brushes can be hung on the walls and clearly marked for the paintshop. Otherwise these tend to go walkabouts.

Both workspaces have now been described in detail, highlighting the minimum needed to get started, as well as a more fully equipped workshop. Where there are financial limitations, there will always be ways of overcoming this, if common sense and intuition are employed. Many of those who have learnt their trade with limited circumstances will find that they are extremely resourceful when it comes to their work, which in the world of technical theatre is a godsend.

List of Essential Health and Safety Equipment/PPE for the Scenic Paintshop

* Ear defenders (these are used when a scenic artist may be required to work in an extremely noisy environment, as well as for using certain tools such as jigsaws, etc. – they are vital).
* Ear plugs (an alternative to ear defenders).
* Dust masks/mist respirator/organic vapour respirator – always check that the correct one is used for a particular job.
* Gloves: disposable, rubber and riggers.
* Kneepads.
* Hard hat (legally required to be worn on specified occasions).
* Steel toe-cap shoes/boots.
* Protective clothing where appropriate (e.g. when working with fibre glass or dyes).
* First-aid kit.
* Fire extinguishers.

4 BASIC JOINTS, MATERIALS, IRONMONGERY AND FIXINGS USED IN SCENIC CONSTRUCTION

This chapter will cover the main joints used in scenic construction: mortise and tenon; lap-halving; and butt. It will also cover ironmongery, such as pin hinges, boss plates, pelmet clips and so on.

By mastering only a few simple procedures, anyone can begin to construct scenery to a professional standard. From understanding the basic principles of timber and steel, to the appropriate joint to be used for a specific application, scenic construction is a field that uses a relatively few techniques to achieve a wide variety of tasks.

The most commonly used material is timber. For basic flat construction, planed softwood is the most appropriate with the most suitable size being 75 × 25mm (3 × 1in). This is available from any good timber yard in a variety of lengths and qualities. In addition to 75 × 25mm, there is a wide range of sizes available to suit any given job. Any good timber yard will be happy to supply the novice with a dimension guide to help make the right choice.

All timber is available in the same standard lengths, these being: 1,800mm (6ft), the shortest standard length, rising in 300mm (1ft) increments to 6,000mm (20ft), the very longest length.

The timber yard sorts its timber into different qualities and prices it accordingly. Factors that affect this sorting include the number of knots in the timber, the straightness of the timber and the actual variety of softwood. Be aware of this when purchasing timber as it can dramatically affect the finish and strength of the construction (not to mention the budget!).

The diagrams overleaf illustrate clearly the various terms relating to timber, it is important to make a note of these as they will be referred to often throughout the book. The most commonly used joints in scenic construction are the mortise and tenon, lap-halving and the butt. The construction of these joints is described overleaf.

Timber Sizing

To avoid confusion, it is important to point out that timber sizes are based on pre-planed dimensions. This means that the finished size of a piece of 75 × 25mm softwood will in fact be closer to 70 × 20mm by the time the timber has been planed or dressed.

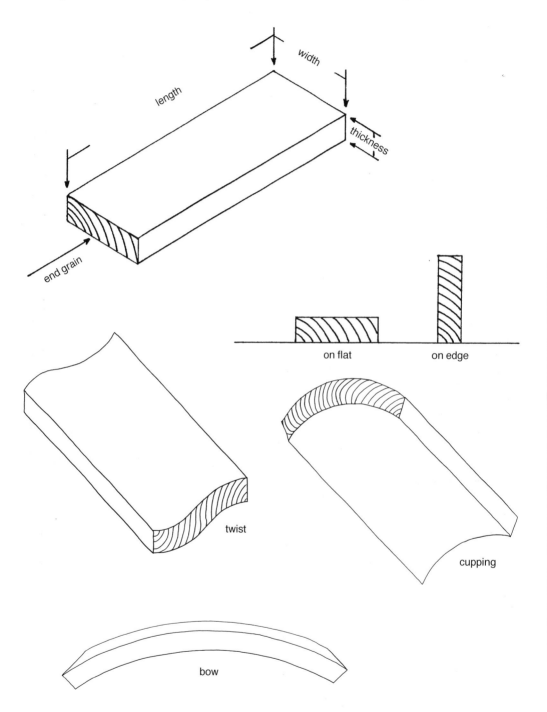

Timber properties. The various terms for each face of timber as well as timber faults.

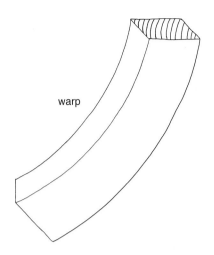

warp

MORTISE AND TENON JOINT

This extremely strong joint is used in most structural framing work such as the construction of a flat or rostrum. The name comes from the two components: the mortise, which is the hole made in one piece of timber; and the tenon, which is the tongue formed on the end of the other.

A standard flat is constructed from a number of different components. Each of these components fits together in such a way so as to make the strongest possible structure in the lightest possible form. Flat construction is discussed in a later chapter but for now, the diagram (right) shows that there are two different joints being used. Although similar, the corner mortise and tenon joint, and the mid-span mortise and tenon joint are constructed in a slightly different fashion.

MID-SPAN MORTISE AND TENON JOINT

In the diagram right, the mid-span mortise and tenon joint is used to join the toggle shoe to the toggle rail. Compare with the mid-span mortise and tenon diagram overleaf and make a note of the different parts of the joint and how they relate to each other.

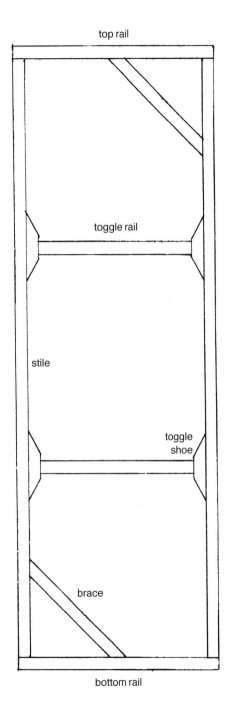

top rail

toggle rail

stile

toggle shoe

brace

bottom rail

A typical flat.

Tools Needed to Construct a Mortise and Tenon Joint

Either:
- combination square
- pencil
- ruler
- marking gauge
- tenon saw
- power drill and assorted drill bits
- 10mm chisel
- mallet
- panel saw
- block plane.

Or:
- combination square
- pencil
- ruler
- marking gauge
- mortising machine
- tenoning machine
- power drill and 8mm bit
- panel saw
- belt sander with medium grade belt.

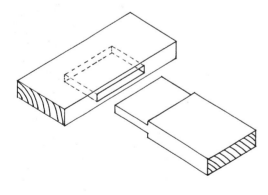

A mid-span mortise and tenon.

Method One

In this example, the tenon is made on the end of the toggle rail. Measure the width of the material that the tenon is to fit into and mark this on the end of the timber, adding an additional 25mm (1in) for wastage. Using the combination square and pencil, extend this dimension around all four sides of the timber.

Now set the marking gauge to half the thickness of the timber, i.e. 10mm (⅜in), and mark the sides and end of the timber. The scribe mark should extend to the limit line that you have already made. To set out the mortise, mark the width of the toggle-rail timber on the edge of the toggle shoe in the desired position. Using the combination square, transfer this position to the opposite edge of the timber.

Using the marking gauge, still set at the same dimension, join the limit lines taking care to mark from the same face – this will ensure a parallel joint. You are now ready to start making the joint. Place the toggle rail on flat in a carpenter's vice. Using the tenon saw, cut along the limit line to the depth of the upper scribed mark. To ensure that you have made a square saw-cut, hold the tenon saw level in the cut and check that the blade is touching the scribe mark on both sides without any curvature or rocking. Turn the timber over and repeat the process on the other side.

Now place the rail on edge in the vice so that it is running upwards in a diagonal fashion – this should expose the end and one edge of the timber. Make sure that the end of the timber is as close as possible to the support of the vice, as this will make the job much easier. Start at the top corner of the timber and saw along the two outer scribe marks until you have reached the furthest corners of the joint. Repeat this process for the inner marks. Now turn the timber over and repeat on the other side. Finally, saw from the end of the timber to the limit line. At this point the waste will fall away leaving the tenon.

To make the mortise, place the toggle shoe on edge in the vice and drill a series of holes with a 10mm drill bit along the marked area taking care to only drill halfway through. Turn the timber over and repeat on the other side. Using the 10mm chisel and mallet, remove the waste, once again taking care to only cut halfway through the timber. Turn the timber over again and complete the cleaning-out process (this procedure is followed to avoid splintering or 'break-out' and ensures a neat joint).

Once satisfied that a square, clean mortise has been made, try the tenon for fit. It should be firm without being over-tight, as this can cause the mortise to split, thus seriously reducing the strength of the joint. If it is too tight, simply pare more of the joint away. Continue with this until satisfied.

Using an 8mm drill bit, drill two holes through the joint, keeping them as far apart as possible. Knock a wooden peg into the holes and remove the excess using a panel saw. The peg should fill the hole completely on both sides of the timber. Sand/plane any remaining waste leaving a smooth face on both sides. The peg forms a very strong means of holding the joint together, whilst at the same time providing an easy means of disassembling. Simply knock or drill the pegs out when you are finished with the set and you will be able to re-use many of the flat components saving time and money in the future. Finally, cut off the tenon wastage using a panel saw, and plane flush.

Whilst the above process will, with care, produce a satisfactory result, it is preferable, where possible, to use woodworking machines to complete the task quickly and efficiently.

Method Two

A number of basic machines will create a tenon with a minimum of fuss. With the correct fences and stops, a band saw or a radial-arm saw fitted with dado cutters will prove more than satisfactory. However, where possible, a tenoning machine is the tool of choice.

A few basic pointers to bear in mind when using this machine:

* Always ensure that the cutting blades are correctly fitted (refer to the owner's manual) and really sharp. Dullness of blade will seriously affect the end result and is dangerous to the operator.
* Fit a spelch block to the cutting fence to prevent break-out of the timber.
* Ensure all safety guards are fitted and correctly adjusted.
* Always wear suitable personal protection equipment. This should include ear defenders and eye protection.
* Keep hands well clear of moving parts when the machine is running.

A tenoner in use. Note the spelch block in correct position.

When using a correctly adjusted woodworking machine, the operator should feel confident that it will produce accurate reproductions every time. Set the end stop to 60mm (the width of the mortise material less 10mm) and clamp the timber into the tenoner. Taking care to follow the above safety tips, firmly pass the timber through the cutting blocks to create a perfect tenon every time. Using the end stop on the tenoner removes the need for any manual marking out, therefore saving large amounts of time in preparation.

Mark out the mortise as per the manual method and mark the centre point using the single pin of the marking gauge. Clamp the timber firmly in the mortising machine and remove the waste material between the limit lines. Always start mortising with the flue of the chisel adjacent to the limit line – this will ensure that the tailings are deposited away from the work area.

With the above procedure complete, assemble the joint in the same fashion as above, using wooden pegs. If available, a belt sander fitted with a medium-grade belt is ideal to remove excess timber and really smooth the joint.

CORNER MORTISE AND TENON

We use virtually the same method as above to build the corner mortise and tenon, with a few important differences. First, the mortise and tenon joint relies on support on all sides to achieve its strength and if timber was removed from one side this would seriously reduce this. To solve this, a haunch is added to the outer side of the joint.

The haunch is approximately two-fifths of the overall width of the joint. It needs to be wide enough to provide the necessary strength on the outer point of the joint but not so wide that it lowers the strength of the tenon itself. As can be seen in the diagram left, the haunch does not extend through the full width of the timber in order to provide maximum torsial strength. A depth of 12mm ($\frac{1}{2}$in) is all that is needed to provide the necessary strength.

Make the tenon in an identical fashion to the mid-span tenon. Once it is cut out, simply mark out the waste area of the haunch and remove it with a tenon saw and mallet and chisel.

To mark out the mortise refer to the stopped mortise and tenon diagram. The mark-out has two extra lines that show the depth and width of the haunch. Note that an extra 25mm (1in) is added on to the end of the mortise to allow for

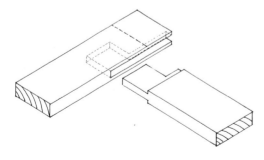

(Above) The mortiser in use.
(Below) Corner mortise and tenon with horn still in place.

wastage. This is called the horn and is removed with a panel saw after the joint is complete and assembled. The purpose of the horn is to provide temporary strength during construction.

To make the mortise using hand tools, first saw along the guidelines to the depth of the haunch. Once this is done, complete the joint as for the mid-span mortise taking care to remove only the area inside the haunch. When this has been done, it is a simple matter to remove the haunch waste with a 10mm (⅜in) chisel. If a mortise machine is available, then it will prove quick and efficient to set the depth stop to the depth of the haunch so that both the full depth cut and the haunch cut can be made at the same time.

A general rule when constructing mortise and tenon joints of either variety with a mortising machine is to stop the tenon 10mm short of the overall width of the mortise material. As well as looking neater, it provides a more robust joint, which is due to maintaining the full integrity of the timber in the mortise material. It provides fewer weak points when the joint is put into active use and is also a more time-efficient method of constructing the joint, i.e. because the mortise is stopped short of the full width, it is not necessary to mortise from both sides. Stopping the joint like this does not affect the strength and the only allowance that needs to be made is when pegging the joint: take care to not place the pegs too close to the end of the tenon.

Haunch Mark-Out

The width of the ruler on a combination square makes an ideal standard haunch width. Hold it flush with the outside edge of the limit line to mark the haunch position. It can also be used on the tenon to mark the waste material.

LAP-HALVING JOINT

The lap-halving joint is often used when flush-joining two pieces of timber and a minimum of machinery is available. The lap-halving joint is a much quicker joint to construct than the mortise and tenon; however, great care must be taken during construction to ensure that the glue bond and the screw penetration is adequate, so as not to affect the overall strength of the joint.

Be aware that the joint lacks innate strength due to the two components having no sideways support. The other matter to bear in mind is that the joint can seriously weaken the timber itself when it is being placed in tension. It is, however, a perfectly suitable joint to use on non-load bearing frames and, in particular, flats that are being clad with plywood, as the plywood will provide additional rigidity to the structure. The author would strongly recommend against using the lap-halving joint in flat construction unless absolutely necessary.

To mark out the timber, simply place the material that is being used as shown in the diagram overleaf (top left). Using a combination square and a sharp pencil to ensure accuracy, mark along all intersecting sides, running a square mark down each side at the limit line. Set a marking gauge to half the depth of the timber and scribe a cutting depth around all sides.

Health and Safety Tip

Never brush the tailings away from around the mortising chisel, it is extremely sharp and can cause a severe laceration. A safer option is to blow the dust away with an airline. Even using a brush is risky, as the bristles can get caught between the auger bit and the chisel, creating potential for bursting of the chisel.

41

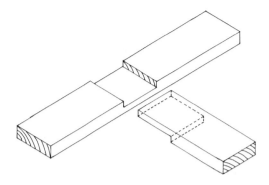

A lapped cross-halving joint.

Cut with a tenon-saw to the marked depth, taking care to saw just inside the limit line. Use a chisel to remove the waste, working from either side of the material to avoid splintering.

It is imperative that both elements of the joint are flat and accurately cut. When satisfied with this, drill two 4.5mm pilot holes into one piece of timber. This hole should be large enough for the screw to pass through easily. Countersink the hole and glue and screw the joint together using 20mm screws. Check that the joint is square and allow it to dry.

The halving joint can also be made on either a radial-arm saw that has been fitted with dado blades or a band saw fitted with a suitable fence and stop.

BUTT JOINTS

Butt joints are by far the quickest and easiest joints to construct, requiring little more than a drill and screwdriver, or even a hammer and nails. The diagrams show a variety of butt joints, which can be used in various applications in scenic construction. The important thing to note is that they have little innate strength and should never be used in high-stress applications. It is advisable to drill pilot holes wherever necessary to avoid the splitting

of timber, thereby reducing further the structural strength.

As well as basic hardware such as screws, nails and hinges, certain specialized items come in handy. With limited space, it is best to show the more useful ones and let the reader apply them as appropriate.

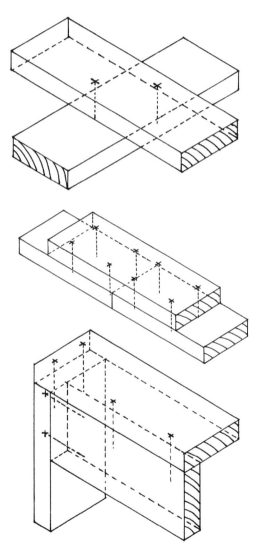

A variety of butt joints.

Ring Plate

A multi-purpose fitting suitable for flying lightweight items and for securing wires and ropes in or off stage.

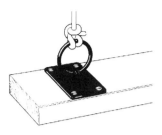

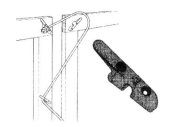

Clummet

The clummet is used to hold two flats together, creating a quick-release mechanism for fast set changes.

Boss Plate

The boss plate is primarily designed as a flush stage fixing. It has a threaded insert to take bolts or thumb screws.

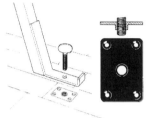

Stud Plate

This is simply a threaded rod or stud welded to a fixing plate. It can be used for fixing together set pieces when access to the rear of the set is restricted. Used when fixing 'flat' to 'flat'.

Peg Plate

Similar to the stud plate and it does the same job, but with the stud welded to the side of the fitting. Used when fixing 'edge' to 'flat'.

Pelmet Iron and Socket

This fitting can be used for fixing pelmets and shelves to flats. The fit is loose enough to be removed quickly for scene changes.

A good alternative is the pelmet clip (not shown), which can be used for drop-in battens or pictures.

Open Grummet

This fitting is used for securing flying wires to the top of flats whilst preventing them from becoming trapped. The wire is twisted at right angles and pulled free. It is designed to guide wires but not to be load-bearing.

Stage Screw

This is used to secure stage braces in place without the need for weights.

A selection of stage ironmongery.

5   FLAT CONSTRUCTION

This chapter looks at the materials, joints and components that go into the construction of a basic flat, and the differences between the construction of a 'hard' covered flat as opposed to the construction of a 'soft' covered flat. The model box is referred to as well as the ground plan and technical drawings, and their uses when commencing a set build are explained. Their relevance to painting will be covered in later chapters. The methods used to construct scenery depend on a variety of factors: the tools available, the requirements of the set and the funds.

TIMBER FLATTAGE

It is preferable to build traditional flats covered in ply or cloth – they are by far the strongest construction as well as being most economical. A standard flat is made up of various components. The two side-pieces are called stiles, these have a corner tenon on each end. The stiles fit into the top rail and bottom rail, which have a corner mortise in each end. These four components form the outer frame of the flat. The toggle rail fits into a pair of toggle shoes by means of mid-span mortises and tenons,

Typical markings on flat components.

44

which in turn are screwed into the outer frame. The toggle shoe is used for two reasons: first, it does not weaken the stile by the removal of timber to form a mortise; and, second, it actually strengthens the stile by effectively forming a splint on the inside of the flat. When a flat is covered or clad with plywood, it is inherently braced laterally through the rigidity of the ply itself. However, when covering a flat with any soft cloth, such as canvas or woollen serge, an additional brace must be used. When the flattage is being covered with canvas or any other painted material, the toggle rails, shoes and braces must be constructed from thinner timber than the outer frame. The inner components can then be set flush to the back of the flat, providing a gap between them and the face of the flat. This prevents adhesion of the cloth to the frame during the priming process. Remember to allow 4–6mm difference in thickness between the outer frame of stiles and rails, and the inner components of toggle rails, toggle shoes and braces; this will be needed later. As a rule, it is a good idea to use 70 × 20mm timber for the inner components and thicker timber for the outer ones.

CONSTRUCTION OF THE FLAT

The diagram on page 37 right shows a typical 1,220 × 3,000mm flat that might be used in any stage play or musical. To make this, first create a cutting list from a working drawing. Since the flat is 1,220mm in width, and the top and bottom rail run the full width of the flat, then by adding 25mm wastage on both ends, a length of 1,270mm is achieved. This should be shown in the cutting list as follows:

top and bottom rails: two at 1,270mm.

To work out the length of the stiles, refer to the construction of a mortise and tenon as described in Chapter 4. Here, the tenon was made 10mm shorter than the overall width of the mortise timber. Therefore, taking into account a joint at both ends of the stile, subtract 20mm from the overall height of the flat. The cutting-list entry will look like this:

stiles: two at 2,980mm.

The toggle rails are worked out in a similar fashion to above. However, because the toggle shoe is fixed to the inside of the stile, subtract twice the width of the stile (i.e. 140mm) from the overall width of the flat. As for the stile, also subtract 10mm for both tenons, therefore arriving at a length of 1,060mm. Bearing in mind that, for a cloth-covered flat, toggle-rail spacings are 1000mm and for a hard-covered flat they are a minimum of 1,220mm spacings, the entry in our cutting list will look like this:

toggle rails: two at 1,060mm.

So, now the cutting list is full (with the exception of the braces and toggle shoes, which are stock items that do not need to be included in the cutting list). The full list should look like this:

top and bottom rails: two at 1,270mm
stiles: two at 2,980mm
toggle rails: two at 1,060mm.

Exercise

Work out a cutting list for a set of four flats that are all 1,150 × 4,000mm. Try setting it out in a similar manner to above and use the simple procedures to arrive at the different lengths. Remember the timber being used is 70 × 20mm PAR (planed all round). Although there are more flats, there should still only be three different lengths. Check at the end of the chapter to see how you got on.

With this basic cutting list, we can look at the generation of other components that go into a standard flat. The toggle shoes and braces are usually mass-produced at quiet times in the workshop. The jigs in Chapter 9 enable rapid mass production of these two items with a minimum of fuss. A basic box set will use several hundred toggle shoes, and time saved in the production period through forward-planning can save many labour hours during the actual build. (*See* Chapter 9 for construction details.)

Once the cutting list has been completed, it is time to start the build process. Remember that the timber has been ordered to suit the job. So, in the case of this cutting list, a minimum of 4,200mm lengths of timber should have been ordered.

Set the end stop to the longest length and, after cutting the feed end off to square, feed the length through to the stop and make your first cut. When the timber is cut to length, mark on it all the information that will be required to successfully construct the flat, i.e. the length, the number or letter of the flat, and the name of the component. It should look something like the photograph on page 44. The writing will also act as a face mark for use in the construction.

Once all the different lengths have been cut, divide them up into tenoned elements and mortised elements. A good rule of thumb is to work on the basis that stiles and toggle rails are usually tenoned and rails are usually mortised. Save double-handling by using a trolley to stack the cutting list and then simply wheel the various components to both the tenoner and the mortiser.

When setting up the tenoner, set the cutting blades to the width of the mortising chisel. Using a metal rule, set the lower blade 5mm above the top of the sliding table: this will set the cutters approximately in the centre of the timber. Do not forget, as long as the face mark is facing up, a nice neat joint will be achieved. Now lock the timber into the tenoning clamp. Make sure to fit a spelch block to the sliding table, this will prevent breakout and create a neater job. Finally, set the end stop at 60mm.

Now, slowly but firmly pass the timber through the tenoner – it is a good idea at this stage to double-check that it is cutting everything just right and that all components will fit correctly. Having completed the first cut, simply turn the length around to complete the tenon on the other end.

Having completed all of the tenons, the rails need mortises. To mark them out, use the skills explained in Chapter 4. Remember to mark out

Radial-Arm Saws and Face Marks

Use a small magnet to secure the cutting-list sheet to the metal arm of the radial-arm saw; it holds the paper in place and will not be affected by dust, like adhesive tape would be! Also remember, always keep the writing or 'face mark' facing upwards when tenoning and outwards when mortising. This will ensure a neat joint at all times and allow for differentiation in timber dimensions.

Safety Tip: Tenoning Dangers

In an industry that is so full of potential dangers, it is vital to take the utmost care at all times. Bearing this in mind, always assess the machine for its own particular dangers. A tenoning machine is a very loud machine, capable of ejecting large pieces of off-cut timber at great speeds. To protect yourself from eye or ear damage, always wear suitable eye and hearing protection when using it.

Safety Tip: Mortising

If possible, have an air gun near by to clear away the wood chips, rather than trying to use fingers or a brush. The bristles of a brush can get jammed between the auger and the chisel, and fingers can be given a nasty nip if they come in contact with the chisel, whether it is moving or stationary.

Incorrectly marked-out haunches (top) – it is easily done! Correct haunches are shown below.

the haunch using a combination square. When marking-out similar components, mark them at the same time using a pair of speed clamps to hold them all together: this will save time and also ensure that they are marked in the same place.

To find the location of the mortise on the edge of the timber, place one of the tenoned components on top of one of the marked mortises, taking care to have both the face marks facing in the same direction. Now mark the position of the tenon on the timber with a sharp pencil. Place this piece in the mortiser and adjust the sliding bed so that the chisel is directly above the marks. Remember to set the depth stops on the mortising machine to allow for the 12mm haunch depth and the 60mm tenon. Due to the varying machines available, refer to the user manual for adjustment directions.

Take a look at the cutting chisel attached to your mortiser: it has a long notch cut up one side. This notch is a flue for disposal of the chips created during the mortising process. When fitting your chisel, it is a good idea to have this flue fitted facing to the right: this will mean that as long as you start mortising from the right-hand end of the joint, the chips will not cover the work surface.

With the pre-checks made, you are ready to start. Take care to keep the work surface clean while mortising, as excessive build-up of wood chips under the work piece will adversely affect the depth of the mortise. Try to get into the habit of keeping one hand on the plunge lever and one on the lateral adjustment wheel. Drop the chisel down into the timber, making sufficient passes to cut out the haunch area. Now disengage the haunch depth-stop and complete the remainder of the joint, overlapping the cuts slightly. Using the air gun when necessary, carefully make the final cut and release the clamp. Slide the timber through the mortiser so that the mortise on the other end is sitting to the left of the clamp. Tighten the clamp and continue the mortising process, remembering to re-engage the haunch depth-stop as appropriate. Following this process makes for fewer interruptions due to depth-stop adjustment.

The tedious job of mortising can be completed relatively quickly and easily, as long as the above directions are followed and, as for all tools, ensure that the cutting elements are really sharp. If the chisel needs sharpening, a reamer can be used to sharpen the edges, whilst a flat file can hone up the auger bit. The mortising completed, the haunches need to be marked out and cut into the tenons. To do this, double-check the depth of the haunch in the mortise and transfer this measurement onto each tenon. A combination square can be adjusted to do this very satisfactorily.

The easiest way to remove the haunch is to cut across the grain with a tenon saw and knock the waste out using a mallet and chisel (very satisfying!). Bearing in mind that the haunch goes on both ends of the stile, it is important they are not marked out on opposite sides of the timber.

TOGGLE RAILS

Next, mark out the position of the toggle rails – remember the different spacings for hard cladding as opposed to soft. If the flat is being covered with any sort of soft material, set the toggle rails equally along the stiles; in this case at 1m intervals. However, if using hard cladding such as plywood, place the toggle rails in the best position to suit the sheet dimensions. As a rule, 2,440 × 1,220mm sheets are used, so it is logical to measure from one end of the flat to a distance of 2,440mm and place the centre of the toggle rail in this position. It is then a simple matter to place the second toggle rail at 1,220mm, providing maximum support and strength. At this stage, it is a good idea to look at toggle-shoe construction.

A toggle shoe, as has already been mentioned, is used to provide extra strength to the length of the stile. A cross-rail housed directly into the stile would substantially weaken the overall structure of the flat creating a very high risk of breakage when standing the flat up. A good rule of thumb is to make the toggle shoe approximately 400mm in length with angled cuts on each end. These make it possible to screw through the edge of the shoe into the stile by means of pre-drilled countersunk holes. Drill the holes about 50mm in from both ends, they should run perpendicular to the back edge of the toggle shoe, providing a method of drawing together shoe and stile. A standard mid-span mortise should be pre-cut into the shoe and a centre line is useful on the side of it. This will make for accurate fixing when constructing the flat.

There are two methods for joining a mortise and tenon joint: either use two metal star dowels driven through from the side of the joint; or, for a less permanent method, wooden pegs can be used. The pegging method has the advantage of strength and semi-permanence. However, for builds where speed is of the essence, the metal dowel can be used. In both cases, try to keep the two fixing points as far apart as possible. Notice in the toggle-shoe diagram, the pegs have been placed diagonally apart without being too close to the edge of the timber where splitting will occur. When using wooden

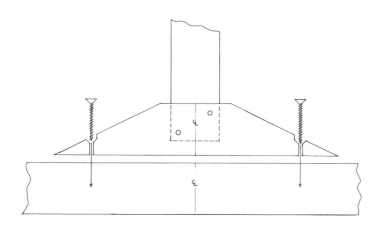

Toggle-shoe diagram showing centre line, peg location, pilot holes, angled ends and mortise.

pegs, drill through the entire joint using sash clamps to hold the work piece firmly in position. Knock the peg through the hole ensuring the peg fills it entirely on both sides and saw off on both sides using a panel saw. Smooth off the peg waste using a belt sander.

To achieve a tight and therefore accurate joint, fit the toggle shoes to their rails prior to flat assembly. With no tension on the joint, it is easier to keep the two components together while pegging or dowelling. With all of the toggle rails and shoes fitted together, divide them into their different flats for ease of construction.

Set up trestles in the approximate shape of the flat that is being constructed and lay the stiles on them. For tall flats, incorporate intermediate trestles for added support. Using a mallet, knock the bottom rail onto one end of the stiles and repeat for the top rail, checking for a tight fit all round. You now have the outer frame of the flat assembled but not fixed together. Prior to fixing, measure the outer diagonals of the flat and adjust so that they are identical. Fix the joints in place using either the pegging method or star dowels, depending on preference. If using the latter, place the joint directly on top of a trestle for maximum support while hammering together. For ease of fixing, place a trestle under each end of the toggle rail and align the pre-marked centre line of the toggle shoe with the mark on the stile. Using 50mm screws, fix the components together drawing them up tight. This will help to straighten any bowing in the timber and make for a neat and accurate flat. Repeat this for all other toggle rails. If covering with soft material, fix the braces on at this stage. The braces should have been pre-cut to a length of 800mm with 45-degree angled cuts on both ends. A countersunk pilot hole drilled in each end makes for ease of fixing and will prevent splitting. Having double checked that the flat is still square, use two 60mm screws to fix the braces in position.

Multiple Flat Construction

When constructing more than one flat of the same size, leave the first flat in position on the trestles once constructed, to act as a pattern for the others. Take extra care to ensure that it is square and accurately constructed and then brace securely in position. It will act as the perfect template for the other flats, as well as supporting the loose components prior to assembly.

Mass production of flattage using the first one as a template.

CLADDING THE FLAT

Now that all of the flats are assembled and fixed in position, it is time to start cladding them. This will vary depending on what is being used as cladding. The easiest way of describing the cladding process is to run through the three main materials used in flat covering. As already discussed, the most common material used these days is 4mm or 6mm plywood. This hardy and rigid material is used in most box sets and is usually finished with a wallpaper or canvas covering for optimum paint finish. As well as a solid finish, it gives a more realistic effect than that of traditional canvas, which can display high levels of wobble around doors and clumsy actors! Also, with

Cutting Sheet Material

To cut a sheet at the correct length, use a straight edge and trimming knife to score the face. Make two firm passes of the knife and place the sheet over the edge of the flat or similar support. Snap it by applying pressure to the face of the sheet and then sharply lifting it quickly and cleanly breaking the sheet.

Toggle Rails and Braces

When cladding with canvas or gauze, under no circumstances should adhesive or staples be applied to the toggle rails or braces. This will result in uneven shrinkage and distortion in the flat. This distortion may manifest itself in a variety of ways including twisting of the flat frame, rippling of the cloth or even by pulling the whole flat out of square.

the prevalence of touring productions, plywood is more resistant to the knocks and rigours that these sorts of productions present. Apply a thin bead of wood glue (approximately 5mm) to the area of the flat frame covered by the first sheet of ply. Now place the ply onto the frame and adjust it so that the narrow end is sitting flush with the bottom rail. Check that the other end sits centrally on a toggle rail. Fix the end of the sheet with 19mm narrow-mouth air staples or 19mm flathead nails every 125mm and 20mm in from the edge. Now assess the long side of the sheet, pull it flush with the side of the flat and start to fix it in a similar manner. If the flat is excessively bowed, it may be necessary to pull the sheet flush a bit at a time. Once the whole edge is fixed and flush, fix the other edges. At this stage, clear any excess glue away from the face of the flat and repeat the process for the remainder. Finally, mark the position of the toggle rails onto the face of the flat and fix at these points as well.

When cladding is complete, use some fine-grade sandpaper to finish the edges.

To cover a flat with canvas or gauze, a different process is needed altogether. Because canvas is a natural material, it will shrink when exposed to moisture. The first step in the painting process involves covering the canvas with a paint mixture called primer. As the primer dries the canvas shrinks tight to the outer frame of the flat providing a smooth uniform surface on which to apply the final paint effects. It is therefore important not to fix the canvas to the flat so tight that as it shrinks it distorts the frame. Bearing this in mind, cut the piece of cloth approximately to size allowing roughly 100mm overhang all round. Lay the cloth onto the flat frame taking care to have the toggle rails flush to the underside of the frame.

Using a staple gun and 6mm wide-mouth staples, start fixing the cloth every 150mm ensuring that the staples are fixed to the inside edge of the frame projecting up slightly from the surface. Work your way along one end and then fix the opposite end, taking care not to pull the cloth too tight. Now fix along the sides pulling the cloth flat but still taking care to keep the tension even rather than too tight. Do not forget to staple on the inner edge of the frame. Fold the flap of cloth back on itself down one edge. Historically, at this stage hot glue would be applied to the frame, however with the advent of latex-based adhesives, this is a thing of the past. Take advice from your theatrical chandler for an appropriate adhesive. Clam 2, Brummer Latex Adhesive is a solvent-free non-flammable adhesive, which provides an exceptionally strong bond; thixotropic, it can be applied by brush or roller and has a long enough open time to allow for working on large areas. After a liberal coat has been applied, fold the cloth back in place and rub it vigorously to force the adhesive into the canvas. Repeat this process around the entire flat. When dry, remove the staples and trim the cloth back from the edge of the flat by approximately 3mm.

This method can be used for canvas, gauze, muslin, calico or any other natural fabric. For man-made cloths, the tension of the cloth must be increased due to the lack of shrinkage.

The final method is used when covering flats with non-painted materials such as wool serge or bolton. These materials are usually used when making masking flats. The low sheen of serge provides excellent properties for masking into wing space, etc., and no theatre should be without a reasonable selection. The flat frame is constructed like a canvas flat with corner bracing and recessed toggle rails. Allow for approximately 150mm overhang all round the flat and place the material on top of the frame. This time pull one end under the frame and staple in place using 6–8mm staples, depending

on the weight of the cloth being used. No adhesive is used and the fabric is pulled tighter than for canvas. This is because it is an unpainted surface and therefore will not be subject to shrinkage. Pull the opposite end tight and once again staple on the underside of the frame. Now flip the flat over so that the back is facing up and start to staple down one side.

It may be necessary to use a hammer to hit home the staples, particularly where the ends are concerned. Stapling from underneath is a tricky job and sometimes it is difficult to apply enough pressure to get a strong fixing. To aid in the process, place a weight such as another hammer on the other side to provide resistance while hitting the staples home. Take care not to pull the material too tight on the first side, as the tightening process should occur on the final side of the flat. To finish the corners, follow the process shown in the illustration below left.

Having completed the stapling process, use a sharp trimming knife to remove the excess cloth. Leave approximately 15mm overhang when completing this task. If it proves difficult, check your blade – it must be really sharp or snagging will occur.

OTHER FLAT CONSTRUCTION METHODS

If all of the machines mentioned in the previous section are available, then it should prove a relatively simple matter to build any required flattage in the above manner. However, these machines are not always at the disposal of the scenic carpenter. When this is the case, several options present themselves. The first is to construct mortise and tenon joints in the handmade manner set out in Chapter 4. However, if time does not permit, then it will be necessary to construct the flattage in one of two relatively quick and efficient methods. Both of these lend themselves far more to flats that are being hard-clad rather than soft-clad.

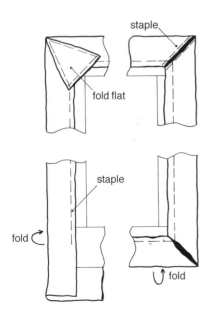

Corner finishing for non-painted materials.

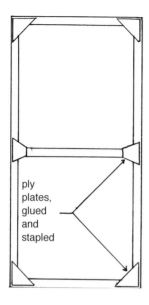

ply plates, glued and stapled

A ply plate flat.

Method one has a similar appearance to the preferred mortise and tenon method with a couple of fundamental differences.

The diagram of a ply plate flat above shows most of the components that we have already covered. We still have two stiles and a top and bottom rail, as well as toggle rails where necessary. However, there are some obvious omissions. Because the flat is covered with plywood,

there are no diagonal braces – the plywood providing all of the lateral bracing. In addition, however, there are no toggle shoes. Remember that the toggle shoes were used in the first method so as to prevent weakening the stiles. So why are they not present here? The reason for this is because, rather than mortising and tenoning the joints, we are simply butting them together.

To make this joint, place the two timber components in position and apply two corrugated fixings or wiggle nails, taking care not to fix too close to the outside of the timber, as splitting may occur. This fixing method holds the frame in place but it is advisable to apply plywood plates at all intersections. (Refer to the diagram below for approximate sizes.) This stabilizes the flat prior to cladding, which should be carried out in the same manner as previously discussed.

The actual construction process involves, first, creating a similar cutting list to that which we have done previously. In light of the slightly different construction, certain factors must be taken into consideration. The top and bottom rails will still run across the full width of the flat but, unlike when creating a mortise and tenon joint, do not allow for wastage and so cut them at 1,220mm. Bearing in mind that butt joints have no point of overlap, the stiles need to be calculated differently. As we are still using 20 ×

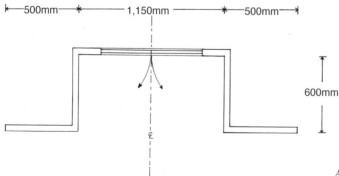

500mm · 1,150mm · 500mm · 600mm

A simple box set ground plan.

70mm PAR softwood, the width of the top and bottom rails need to be subtracted from the overall dimension of the flat. To avoid confusion, assume the flat is 3,000 × 1,220mm, as earlier in the chapter. This will mean that the stiles should be 3,000mm minus 140mm (i.e. twice 70mm): the stiles should measure 2,860mm. Finally, the toggle rails should measure the width of the flat minus the width of two stiles. This will mean that they are 1,220mm minus 140mm making them 1,080mm in length.

Once the cutting list has been made, cut the components out as before. If a radial arm saw is not available, use a panel saw or tenon saw.

A common mistake is to measure and mark all of the components consecutively along a length of timber prior to cutting. This should be avoided, as the width of the saw blade will reduce the length of the next piece creating inaccurate work. It is better to mark a length and cut it off prior to cutting the next piece.

Mark out the positions for the toggle rails along the length of the stiles. Remember to mark all of the stiles at the same time, so as to ensure consistency. Lay the frame components out on trestles, as for the previous flat construction. Nail two corrugated fixings into each joint, as already discussed, and strengthen the joint by nailing a 4mm ply plate at each joint using wood glue and 20mm flathead nails. Once the flat frame is fixed together, check that it is square by measuring the diagonals corner to corner. If they measure the same, then the frame is square. Fix ply to the face in the same manner as before.

The final method used in flat construction is a variation on a construction method used in television and film construction. The flats are constructed out of either 70 × 20mm or 45 × 20mm but, unlike the two previous methods, the timber is placed on edge and screwed together. This is a very quick method of construction and is ideal when the set involves a lot of openings, such as windows, doors and alcoves.

Typical butt joints used in a flat built on edge.

The disadvantage of this sort of construction is in the thickness of the flat itself. With the timber on edge, it creates a structure nearly three times as thick as a conventionally constructed flat. This will impact considerably on storage of the flattage, as well as the actual construction of the set. However, where storage space is not a problem (a situation that the author has never been fortunate enough to encounter!) or when the set is not being kept after the run of the production, it is a method that has its advantages.

Next consider the construction of a standard 3,000 × 1,220mm flat. Try working out the cutting list for the flat, bearing in mind that the top and bottom rails run the full width of the flat with no overhang. In addition to this, the toggle rails butt into the stiles, meaning that two times 20mm must be subtracted from the overall width of the flat to arrive at their length. Follow the same procedure for the length of the stiles. Once again, cut the timber out, referring to the cutting list, and place similar components together. Mark out the position of the toggle rails and, using a 4.5mm drill bit and drill, pre-drill two holes at each position on the stiles, as well as at each end of the top and bottom rails. Countersink the holes and fix together using 50 × 4mm countersunk wood screws. Check for square and clad, as discussed previously. It may be preferable to fix any toggle rails that are on a sheet joint, on flat rather than on edge, as this will provide greater surface area for fixing.

WORKING FROM THE GROUND PLAN AND MODEL BOX

Having considered the various methods of flat construction, the next step is to apply them to an actual set. The task is to build a fairly standard set that could be seen in any proscenium arch theatre. The generic name for such a set is a box set, so called because it usually forms three sides of a room with the imaginary fourth wall between the audience and the actors. But where to begin? To answer this, consider the model box from the perspective of the audience. With the ground plan and any available designer's drawings at hand, assess how the set will be perceived from the auditorium. From a structural perspective, there must be no 'light leaks'

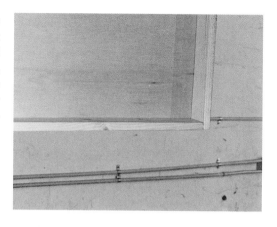

A flat on edge showing joint detail.

visible, which means cracks of light that show between two flats from backstage.

A rule of thumb is to always have the upstage/downstage flats butting into the face of any cross-stage flats, whilst keeping all external corners mitred to ensure a neat joint.

Having done this, the true lengths of the various flats need to be assessed. As an example, look again at the ground plan on page 52. The flat in the upstage corner runs past the upstage/downstage flat but the designer has shown only its internal dimension. If the flat were built to this dimension, a corner would be left (as shown in the diagram below).

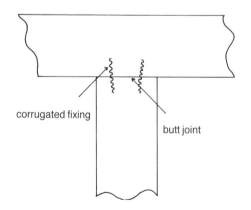

Typical butt joint used in flat built with corrugated fixings.

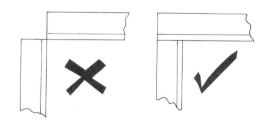

Two flats in a corner without enough length to run past each other and two with enough to compensate.

To rectify this, add the thickness of the intersecting flat to the overall length to allow for proper construction. Taking into account that 20mm-thick timber and 4mm-thick plywood is being used, add an extra 24mm as cover when a flat runs behind another intersecting flat. For instance, the flat described here has an internal dimension of 1,150mm but, because it runs behind the upstage/downstage flat, an additional 24mm must be added to allow for overhang.

Try doing this on the ground plan. This needs to be done prior to completing any cutting list, as it will dramatically affect the final outcome.

Now that the ground plan has been checked for overhanging flattage, refer back to the drawings given at the beginning of the production process: these are called the designer's drawings rather than technical drawings because the drawings that the carpenter receives from the designer may not have all of the information that is required to build the set accurately. The designer's job is to show how the finished set should look but does not need to take into account the construction process.

Now that the pre-build checks are complete, any technical drawings that are necessary to complete the build accurately need to be drawn. It is best to draw these to the same scale as that of the designer's drawings, usually 1:25. For regular rectangular flattage, it is not necessary to redraw them, as it is a simple matter to adjust the cutting list; however, for door flats or irregular shapes, it is advisable to do so. This leads on to the next chapter, which covers the construction of doors and windows, as well as the flattage that they fit into.

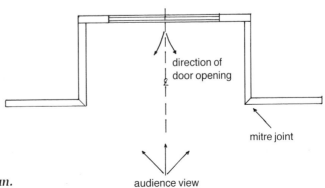

Correct flat layout on ground plan.

direction of door opening

mitre joint

audience view

6 DOOR CONSTRUCTION

This chapter will cover the construction of solid doors, as well as the construction of hollow doors. Particular attention will be paid to the allowance for lock and hinge blocks in hollow-door construction. The construction of hollow panelled doors will be covered, as well as the fitting of mouldings, locks and hinges. Also, at this stage, the construction of straight and curved door reveals will be touched upon.

The important thing to bear in mind when building a door for the stage, is how it will sound when it shuts. The light hollow clunky sound of a badly constructed door will instantly give the game away and remind the audience more of daytime television soap opera rather than highbrow Ibsen. Assess the uses of the door in the play and choose the appropriate construction method. The average farce will give even the strongest door a good workout, and often specific requirements are made of a door such as locks, keys, door handles and hinges. Very often, oversized or period doors are required, which, if built solidly, would be unmanageable for stage crew, as well as placing excessive stress on door-jambs and suchlike. The carpenter should be clear about all of these matters prior to commencement of the building process.

Building a door can be approached in a variety of different ways, with the three most common methods being hollow construction, hollow panelled and solid construction. These three methods all present different advantages, as well as disadvantages, which will be examined in this chapter. The experienced carpenter will quickly know when to apply each specific method to the door at hand.

Light in weight, as well as being cheap and reasonably quick to construct, the hollow door has many useful applications. Of all the doors, it is by far the easiest to construct, with or without power tools or wood machines. It does, however, run the risk of having a hollow sound when being opened and closed. When built correctly, this problem can be overcome simply and effectively.

Hollow Doors

With the ever-spiralling interest in DIY, it is now very often possible to buy hollow doors from your local builder's hardware. Try comparing the difference in price between one of these factory built doors as opposed to the materials involved in constructing one from scratch. On a major build, it may be worth spending the extra money and saving valuable build time by supplying doors in this manner.

HOLLOW-DOOR CONSTRUCTION

This is the quickest and easiest method of construction, used most commonly in plays set in modern times or when *trompe l'oeil* painting effects are being used.

To build a hollow door, select straight lengths of 50 × 25mm PAR softwood. It is important that the timber is as straight as possible because it needs to fit into a jamb (the frame from which the door hinges). Warped or bowed timber will stop the door opening and shutting correctly and may create light-leaks.

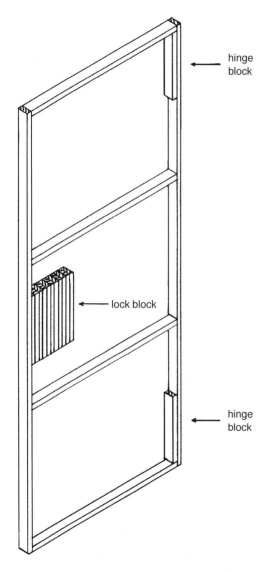

A hollow door-frame showing lock and hinge blocks.

To check the straightness of a piece of timber, hold it from one end and sight along the length. Any curve or bend will become apparent. This practice is particularly important when building doors or windows where the effect of bowing is most pronounced.

Having checked for bowing, set the timber to one side in order to complete a cutting list.

Working from the diagram (left), prepare a cutting list for the construction of a standard 760 × 1,980mm door. Bear in mind that the finished dimensions of the softwood after it has been planed should finish around 45 × 20mm. As a rule, it is a good idea to run the stiles the full height of the door, as it looks neater and, as there is no end-grain, it makes it easier to plane should any adjustments be necessary. It is a simple matter to work out the cutting list: the stiles being 1,980mm (full door height), the rails are the overall width minus twice the thickness of the timber, and it is wise to allow for an additional two intermediate cross-rails to add rigidity and strength. Working on the principle that the timber is 45 × 20mm, subtract 40mm from the width of the door, leaving 720mm. Take care to allow for a lock block, which should be made from the same timber and extend 50 mm beyond the depth of the door furniture.

Without the lock block, there will be nothing but 4mm ply to fix handles to, possibly leaving the actor with a doorknob in their hand and no means of escape! It is a good idea to cut a number of blocks to the same length, and glue and clamp them together prior to constructing the actual door, this will allow for the glue to dry in time for when it is needed. Having done this, cut the door components out carefully and mark the positions of the rails on the stiles.

Be sure to mark out both the stiles at the same time for greater accuracy. Set out the frame elements on a flat surface and, using a pair of sash clamps to hold them in position, drive a pair of 75mm panel pins through the stile into the rails

57

at all points of contact. Take a nail punch and drive the nails well into the timber to allow for any additional fitting requirements.

Using 4mm ply, cut two sheets approximately 20mm larger than the overall size of the door in both directions, e.g. 2,000 × 780mm, and, having applied a 5mm bead of wood adhesive to one side of the frame, carefully lay the ply on to it. As when cladding flattage, start with one edge of the sheet on a narrow side and fix every 100–150mm with panel pins or, preferably, narrow-mouth staples. Now pull the frame square up one of the long sides, fixing as before. If the corner of the sheet matches the corner of the flat, then it is likely that the door will be square. Finish fixing down the

A router fitted with edge-trimming bit.

Door Facing

It is a common mistake to face only the side visible to the audience with doors that open offstage. This will make the door less solid and tend to lead to the door flexing excessively. The end result of this will be the door bouncing in the jamb. When working in repertory, it is not uncommon to put doors into stock, so it will make for a more versatile door if it is finished on both sides.

---

other two sides and across the intermediate rails, tidying up the edge with either a block plane or, if available, a router and edge trimming bit.

Turn the door over and glue the door block in position, leave for 10 min while the adhesive goes 'off' and, when ready to apply the second sheet, apply more adhesive to the top face of the block, as well as the frame itself. Repeat the nailing/stapling process for the second side and trim as before. Finally, aris the edges of the door and give a light sand to ensure a splinter-free surface.

Different periods have produced different architectural features, one of the most obvious of these is the door and, more specifically, the panelled door. Before the advent of sheet materials such as plywood and hardboard, it was necessary to construct doors from solid uprights and cross-members with small panels inserted into the spaces left over, hence the name for this style of door. Although fashions do not have a specific start and cut-off date, Georgian, Victorian and Edwardian period doors all have slightly different features and it is important for the scenic carpenter to understand them.

As can be seen, the major differences manifest themselves in the number of panels and the style of mouldings incorporated in the finish. All of the above can be built using the same techniques as presented in the next section. As

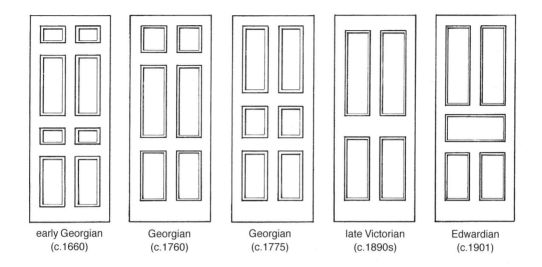

| early Georgian (c.1660) | Georgian (c.1760) | Georgian (c.1775) | late Victorian (c.1890s) | Edwardian (c.1901) |

Historical changes in door styles through the ages.

with much of scenic construction, a few basic principles can be applied in a variety of ways. So, now to consider the most theatrical way to construct a door using a few simple practices. Rather than using solid timber to construct a door, which will be heavy and expensive, a lightweight frame can be made up that can be clad with 4mm ply to create the appearance of a panelled door. To finish off the effect, the panelled areas are filled in with 6mm ply to create a lightweight, durable, low-cost stage door.

HOLLOW-PANELLED DOOR CONSTRUCTION

To construct a basic four-panel door, first construct the outer frame. To provide the finished result with the desired light weight, use 25 × 50mm PAR software. This has finished dimensions of 20 × 45mm and makes the ideal framing material. Before starting the construction, make up a cutting list for the door.

The door needs to finish up looking like it is constructed from three solid uprights and three similarly solid cross-members. But do not forget that this door is for the stage and, therefore, the components are not what they seem. Each of the cross-members and uprights will actually be hollow boxes that are covered with 4mm ply. So, to start the cutting list, allow two lengths of 25 × 50mm PAR software for each component. All of the cross-members will be the same length, i.e. the overall width of the door minus 40mm, which is the thickness of the two outer edges of the door. Therefore, six lengths at 740mm are required. Six uprights will also be needed but the two outermost lengths will be the full height of the door, i.e. 2,000mm, whilst the four internal lengths will be less the thickness of the top and bottom edges of the door, i.e. 1,960mm. This should become clearer by looking at the diagram overleaf. The door-frame itself, before it has been clad, looks like a number of ladders with irregularly spaced rungs contained within an outer frame.

The outer frame is constructed in an identical fashion to the flush panel door, however, before assembly, it is a good idea to do a mark-out for the internal panels. As with flat construction, it is a good idea to clamp the matching components together to do the mark-out, ensuring that all the lengths are correct and sitting flush and square with each other.

To construct the door, it is necessary to remove half the thickness of each internal component wherever it intersects with another component. To work this out, work from the drawing showing the dimensions of the door. Measure the distance from the bottom of the door to each edge of the cross-members. Make a note of this and then do the same starting from one side of the door, this time measuring the distance to each upright. Transfer these measurements onto the outer frame components

and, where relevant, the internal members. Remember to place a locating cross on the correct side of your marks.

Having done the mark-out, next remove half of each internal joint to leave a slightly unusual halving joint behind. Obviously, this is not necessary for the joints that occur on the outer edges of the door and, indeed, these are simple butt joints.

Glue all the joints prior to fixing and use two 50mm panel pins on the outer joints and a single 40mm pin to hold the internal joints in place.

Finally, prior to cladding, it is necessary to cut short fixing blocks wherever the horizontal cladding strips finish; this is because the vertical strips will not allow for end-fixing for the horizontal strips.

Having done this, measure the overall width of each of the 'rails' and 'uprights' and cut strips of ply to these sizes. The strips are fixed to the frame so that the grains of the strips match the grain as it would appear in a solid door. Fix the strips with panel pins and adhesive.

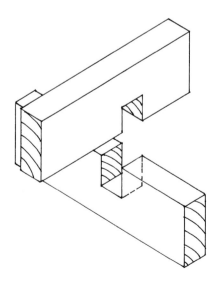

An unclad panelled door frame.

Detail of mark-out.

Remember to fix a lock block in the appropriate position prior to cladding the second side of the door. Also, add an additional block of 25 × 50mm at the top and bottom of the hinged side of the door, to allow for their fixing. Bearing in mind that softwood is the most commonly used timber in the theatre, it needs as much strength in depth as possible.

Using a router and rebate cutter, set the router to slightly over half the thickness of the door and form a rebate in all of the panel openings. It will be necessary to square off all of the corners using a sharp chisel. This done, measure and cut 6mm ply panels to fit and fix in place, using wood glue and panel pins.

Now it is time to fit one side of the door with an appropriate panel moulding. These come in a variety of profiles and dimensions; this should be confirmed with the designer prior to building.

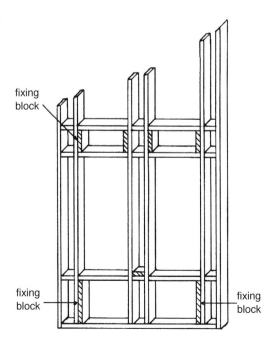

Blocks for horizontal strip fixing.

fixing block

fixing block

fixing block

The fixing of the moulding should be a fairly straightforward matter, but great care must be taken to ensure an accurate finish. The principle is to cut the selected moulding to the same length as the horizontal and vertical sides of each panel. An internal 45-degree cut is made on each end of all the pieces, so that when they are placed in the panel opening, the corners create what is known as a mitre joint. This joint takes some time to perfect when using a tenon saw freehand, however there are many useful saw guides available to aid the novice in this pursuit. As with all areas of scenic construction, this is a skill that improves with practice. A light plane with a block plane will improve the finish of the joint; however, be careful not to compound any minor errors by overworking it.

When measuring the length of the various pieces of panel moulding, subtract 1mm from each dimension. This will allow for a slightly easier fit. Fix the moulding in position by either using an appropriate length panel pin or air nail. If a really good fit has been made, it may even be possible to hold the mouldings in place simply with wood adhesive. Ensure that all of the components fit before starting to fix them in position, as slight adjustments usually need to be made. With one side of the panels finished, repeat the process for the other. Bear in mind that due to the routing-out of the rebates, the panels will be different dimensions on both sides.

With all of the moulds fitted and in place, give the edges a final aris and sand for a thoroughly believable 'solid' door.

SOLID PANELLED DOOR

When the occasion arises for a solid panelled door, it is important that the scenic carpenter knows how to set about constructing one. Using our old friend the mortise and tenon, it is a relatively simple matter to create a sturdy door for a fraction of the cost of a bought door.

This assumes that the workshop has a mortiser and either a tenoner or a band saw. Either of these tools will create a tenon, indeed even a radial-arm saw fitted with dado cutters will do the job.

Under no circumstances should the thickness of the door be stinted on. An optimum thickness is 38mm, which when planed finishes at approximately 32mm. The reason it is so important to maintain adequate thickness is to ensure vital strength for the hinges.

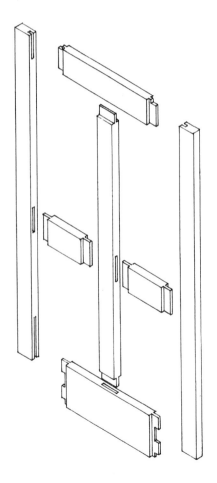

An exploded diagram of a solid panelled door showing detail of rails and all joints.

Actors have a nasty habit of mistreating doors on stage and the extra stress and strain that they receive during the run of a show can literally split them in half. This said, the width of the rails and uprights vary depending on the period of the play and the designer's wishes.

The Construction Process

The cutting list for a door similar to the solid panelled door above needs to take into account the position of the joints and how they combine to create the finished article. Looking at the diagram (left), it can be seen that the mortises need to be cut into the stiles and the tenons are all made on the ends of the rails. The only exception to this is for the central upright, which is mortised into the top and bottom rails. Wherever possible, the mortise and tenon should be a stopped joint with the mortise set to stop 10mm short of the width of the timber. Where two rails meet in the central upright, this will not be possible. Instead they must run 5mm short of half the width of the upright. Usually, the bottom rail tends to be much wider than the rest of the components, this is for aesthetic reasons, making it impossible to make a full-depth joint. This should not cause any problems and a 60mm deep joint will serve the purpose very well.

Using the above information and the diagram, try working out the cutting list for the door.

Mark out your components in exactly the same way as you would for any other mortise and tenon joint, remembering haunches for the corners and mid-span joints where appropriate. The exception to this is found in the joint used for the bottom rail to the uprights. Because of the extreme width of the rail, it is not practical to create an entire mortise and tenon, so instead two smaller ones are made, maintaining a haunch all the way across. The easiest way to describe this is by diagram. Note that the haunch is kept where a tenon has not been positioned: this provides strength and rigidity to the joint without the door being weakened by excessive removal of timber.

Now that all of the components are cut out, it is important to assemble the inner section of the door first, prior to adding the top and bottom rails and finally adding the outer uprights. Having glued all of the joints with wood adhesive, clamp the frame firmly together using sash clamps, taking care to set the door down flat during the drying time, and check that the door frame is square.

Use wooden pegs to fix the joints in place and finish by planing and sanding all discrepancies.

At this stage, the door is ready to be panelled as per the hollow-panelled construction above. Follow these instructions to finish with a solid professional door that will withstand the most antisocial of cast members.

In conclusion, all of the above methods of door construction will provide the vital elements for a satisfactory end result. They all provide a rigid frame to hold the door straight and true, in addition they all have provision for the

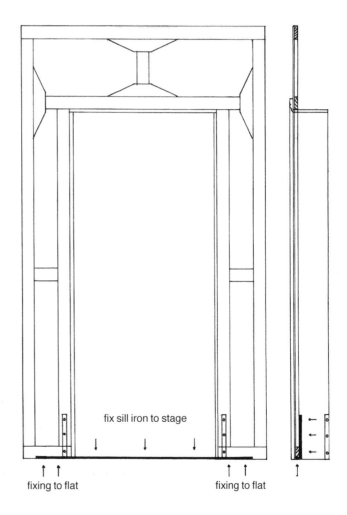

Door-flat construction.

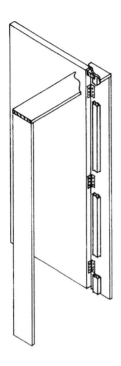

Cutaway diagram of door hung in door jamb and reveal.

and any reveal. The jamb is a three-sided frame that the door fits in to create the doorway. The components are shown in the diagram (left).

These days, a jamb is usually only 125mm to 150mm wide, however in period construction, it is often necessary to place this jamb in a reveal, which is a small return that surrounds the doorway suggesting wall thickness. When this is required, either a width of 18mm ply will do the job or, in extreme circumstances, a small flat-like construction will do the job. The jamb is fixed into the reveal to create greater strength and also to provide the door with greater rotation if opening through the doorway.

As can be seen from the photograph below, because the doorway is not actually fixed to the

Clandestine Marriage *doorway from behind. RADA, Director Peter Oyston, designer Julie Nelson.*

fixing of hinges and fitting of locks, as well as a solid quality when the door is being closed.

The diagram (*see* previous page) shows the necessary alterations to a standard flat to allow for a door-opening. As can be seen, the construction itself is identical; however, note the locations of mid-span and corner mortise and tenons. Also, calculate the exact location of the door-opening in the flat prior to construction. The width of the door is already known, so simply measure the thickness of the material that will be used to form the reveal and door jamb, and add these together. It is important to add an extra 3mm on either side of the door to allow it to close freely in the jamb, and add an extra 15mm to the overall height of the opening for the same reason.

With the door constructed to the required size, it is time to look at building the door jamb stage, a device called a sill iron is used to hold the door jamb straight and true. Usually it will fix into the back of the jamb and, as its name suggests, it is made from metal. For large reveals, a reveal iron, which will actually fit onto the back of the flat, is used to support it.

There are far too many different door handles and fittings to go into in this book; however, as in all areas of aesthetics, the designer should always be consulted prior to the selection of any of the above. The fitting of hinges is another matter. The usual hinge used in scenic construction is a lift-off hinge. This handy hinge comes in left- and right-handed pairs and, as the name suggests, comes apart enabling the door to be removed from the jamb for scene changes or easy storage. Lift-off hinges are available in 75mm or 100mm sizes, with the larger size being more suitable for larger, heavier doors. For most lightweight doors, two hinges will be more than adequate. However, it may prove appropriate to add a central hinge for particularly tall doors: this will help to keep the door running straight and true, as well as spreading the weight uniformly.

Prior to fitting the hinges it is important to back off the inside edge of the door to prevent the door binding in the jamb. To do this, scribe a 2mm line along the back edge of the door and clean off using a smoothing plane. With the backing-off of the door complete, the next step is to fit the hinges. Measure 150mm from the top of the door to the top of the upper hinge and 225mm from the bottom of the door to the bottom of the lower hinge.

Place the hinge flat on the door with the knuckle of the hinge sitting against the edge of the door. With a very sharp pencil, mark the outline of the hinge, this will provide an accurate template with which to start to house the hinge into the door. Now measure the overall thickness of the hinge when both plates are running parallel to each other.

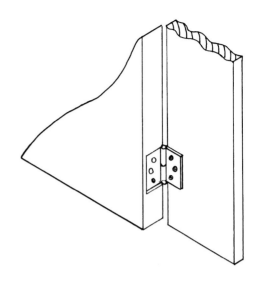

Detail showing hinge housed fully into door and fitted flat onto the door jamb.

Using a marking gauge, scribe the depth onto the edge of the door between the hinge limit lines. Normally the hinge would only house in half its depth, however in the theatre the tendency is to house it the full depth because it means that the jamb will not need housing as well. Using a sharp 25mm chisel, position the blade across the grain, just inside one of the limit lines with the bevel of the chisel facing into the hinge. Knock the blade down to the depth marked on the side of the door. Repeat this process for the other end and carefully cut along the length of the hinge-housing taking care not to split the door along the grain. Now make a series of shallow angled cuts with the chisel down to the depth of the housing and carefully clear away the waste.

Fit the hinges to the door with 40mm screws. It is a good idea to use only half of the available holes initially, to allow for corrections where necessary. To hang the door, set it in the jamb and wedge it up to within 3mm of the top.

When hanging a door, to achieve a regular gap, lay a pair of 75mm nails on top of the door prior to wedging up. Failure to do this may result in the door binding with the head of the reveal. Mark the position of the hinges with a sharp pencil. With the door sitting at 90 degrees to the opening, screw the hinges in position with screws to suit. Now that the door is hung in the jamb, it is time to fit the doorstop. With the door in its closed position, fit the header piece of stop so that it sits 2mm away from the door on the hinged side and flush with the door on the handle side. Now fit the upright pieces once again with the hinged side sitting 2mm away from the door and the handle side running hard up against the inside of the door. This will prevent the door from binding when closing and will allow for paint as well.

A fully functional door, jamb and reveal has now been achieved, with the exception of door handles. Now it is a good idea to cover a few tips for effective installation of a door flat.

* Always ensure that the flat and door are running vertically or plumb. Use a spirit-level or plumb-bob to make sure that the door will close properly and not 'creep' (move on its own) when left ajar.
* Give the door flat plenty of support to stop wobbles when the door is in use. Either a stage or French brace on either side of the opening will be ideal.
* Occasionally, doors develop a mind of their own, moving at unwanted times. A simple trick that can be used when the door opens offstage is to fix an old 25mm paint brush to its bottom. The bristles will hold the door in position but will still allow the door to be used in a normal fashion.
* Another way to reduce unwanted movement in door flats is to position the openings near the corner of a room. If this is not possible, a reveal or return flat near the doorway will also add rigidity.

CURVED REVEALS

To create a more exotic feel in a play, many designers ask for curved or profiled reveals – a technique that is often necessary when working on pantomime or period plays. The *Arabian Nights* or the *Jew of Malta* is not going to look convincing being performed on a set with ordinary square doors and windows. Whilst it is a simple matter to cut a curve out of a piece of ply, it is another matter to create a doorway with the appearance of thickness. Indeed, in days gone by it was necessary to use materials such as skin ply to create the curve. The problem was that to achieve the desired curves, the ply needed to be extremely thin, severely compromising its strength. With the development of Flexi-ply, a highly flexible and very strong material, this no longer presents a problem. An example is considered here. To construct a curved reveal of 250mm in depth and with a radius of 400mm, apply some simple sums. Flexi-ply of 5mm is available in 2,440 × 1,220mm sheets and can be bought in long-grain and short-grain sheets. The long-grain sheets are ideal for building canons, trees and rockets and suchlike, whilst the short-grain sheets are more suitable for circular rostrum skirts, barrels and, indeed, curved door reveals.

To create the reveal, it is first necessary to establish the overall width of the opening in the flat frame. To do this, add twice the thickness of the Flexi-ply to the overall opening of the door. Use this measurement when constructing the flat frame, adding an additional 5mm to the overall height of the opening as well. Fix a square reveal to the back of the opening using 18mm ply – it should be exactly the same size as the opening in the flat and will provide support for the Flexi-ply. Cut out two pieces of 18mm ply to the width of the opening and set up a circle jig on the router (*see* Chapter 9). Find the centre-point along one of the long sides and fix the routing jig in position. By setting the router so that the outside of the blade is in line with the edge of the ply, a perfect semicircle is created that will act as a former for the reveal. This can be fixed in position into the door opening creating a uniform fixing point for the reveal to follow. Make sure that a second former is cut to support the back of the reveal Cut a strip of Flexi-ply to the depth of the reveal (250mm) and fix it in position. Clad the flat with the required thickness of ply, over-sailing the arch. Finally, with an edge trimmer fitted in the router, cut out the waste from the centre of the opening. This will leave a perfect archway and reveal. This method can be applied to any shaped arch reveal, as well as fireplace openings, windows and bulkheads.

Matching plywood circles act as formers for a circular window reveal.

Clad the reveal first and then cover the flat with 4mm ply.

7 TREAD CONSTRUCTION

We will look at the difference between closed-tread and open-tread construction, and the provision of handrails and balustrades. A detailed examination of the setting out of the tread and riser will be covered including ideal dimensions. We will also look at the construction of useful space-saving get-off treads, as well as ladders and single treads.

In the theatre, stairs and staircases are referred to as 'treads'. As in real life, they perform a variety of functions. The simplest type is solid or block construction, often used as a means for actors to exit from a raised stage level. When used in this context, they are called 'get-off' treads. It can be a relatively simple procedure to construct a set of 'get-offs'; however, it is important to take into account several points first. The most important of these is the space available, both in width and length, to the side of the set. It is also important to establish the following:

* How many actors need to use the treads at once?
* Do they need to exit quickly?
* Are there any scene changes that will be affected by having a large set of get-offs in the way?
* How will they affect the health and safety of the backstage area?
* Do they need handrails?

All of these issues need to be solved before the commencement of construction.

The two important terms to understand at this point are 'going' and 'riser'. The going is the depth of the actual tread from the front to the back and the riser is the height from the top of one tread to the next.

As a rule, it is a good idea to make the going about 250mm and the riser 175mm. This makes for a safe and comfortable set of treads that will make the actor's job much easier. It is extremely important that the tread and riser stay consistent. Not only will they be much easier to walk up and down, and look more 'real life', but irregular treads, particularly as get-offs, are very dangerous and could result in serious injury. The above measurements will vary from time to time, however they provide a good starting point.

BUILDING SOLID OR BLOCK TREADS

To establish the actual dimensions of the treads, it is necessary to carry out a simple survey. First, measure the overall height of the rostrum or staging to which the treads have to rise. For the purposes of this example, the height is 640mm and there is plenty of space offstage for the treads to run, so all that is left to do is to divide the height into comfortable tread intervals. Remember the normal tread height is 175mm, so simply divide the overall height of 640 × 175mm. The result is 3.6571429! This means that approximately 3.6 treads at 175mm will fit into this set of get-offs. Obviously this is highly impractical, not to mention dangerous, so instead divide 640mm by 4, the next round number above 3.6571429. This gives a riser height of 160mm, which is still very comfortable to climb. Working from this point, it is possible to establish that this set of get-offs will be comprised of four treads of 240mm in depth with 160mm risers and, due to the lack of restrictions in space, they will be a useful width of 1,220mm.

The materials that are commonly used in get-off construction are 75 × 25mm PAR softwood and 18mm plywood. The plywood forms the bulk of the treads with the softwood acting as stiffeners and bracing. The first task is to mark-out the stringers or sides of the get-offs. These are generally constructed from 18mm plywood.

In light of the width of the treads, it will be necessary to have a mid-span supporting stringer to reduce flex in the structure. The diagram below shows the finished mark-out of the stringers, which has been done using a roofing square. It is necessary, when marking-out, to subtract the thickness of the first tread from the overall dimensions. Therefore, if the first riser is 160mm, subtract 18mm from it leaving 142mm. From this point continue to mark out the treads and risers sequentially until the final tread, when it will be necessary to subtract

Accurate Mark-Outs

As is clear from the diagram below, the overall length of the stringer will be 18mm less than the length of the actual set of treads, so in this case the stringer length will be 702mm. To make the mark-out process easier and more accurate, cut the timber to length beforehand. This provides an excellent method for checking the accuracy of the mark-out because if it does not fit on to the sheet, then it is not right!

18mm for the last riser. Look closely at the diagram to fully understand this slightly complicated instruction.

With the first stringer marked out, repeat for the other side and the mid-span stringer. Very often it is possible to mark out another stringer on the opposite side of the sheet, saving material and therefore money.

Using a jigsaw carefully cut out the stringers, taking extreme care to follow the line exactly. As these will form the support of the treads, a stable base can be made by cutting the bulk of

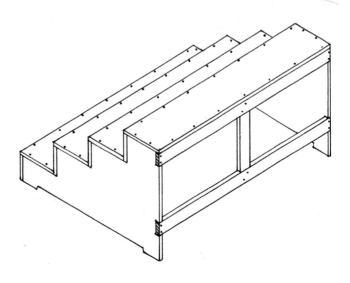

Solid tread construction including details of foot cut-outs.

the timber away from the base leaving a set of feet on which the treads will rest. In addition, mark-out at the top of each stringer, and also 100mm from the bottom, a 70 × 20mm notch to house the softwood stiffeners. Double-check the dimensions of the actual softwood to be used, as these vary from timber yard to timber yard. Cut these out also using the jigsaw and ensure that all edges are sanded and clear of splinters and sharp edges.

The next step is to cut out the actual treads and risers. Once again, the material that will be used is 18mm plywood. At this stage it is a good idea to work out the cutting list. All of the treads will be 240 × 1,220mm in length but the risers will be slightly different.

The bottom riser will be 142mm, allowing for the 18mm tread sitting on top of it, to make it up to 160mm. However, the other treads will actually be 160mm. This is because, as is clear in the diagram, to gain maximum strength the riser runs from down behind the tread to underneath the tread above. Therefore, the cutting list should read as follows:

four of 1,220 × 240mm (treads)
three of 1,220 × 160mm (risers)
one of 1,220 × 142mm (bottom riser).

Notice the length of the treads and risers. What measurement does 1,220mm correspond to in standard material sizes? Of course, it is the width of a standard sheet of plywood. To make the treads neat and regular, work across the sheet when cutting them out. This avoids extra cutting to length, as well as any potential for inaccuracies.

The assembly of the get-offs themselves is a straightforward one. First, clamp the stringers upright in position on a workbench. Having cut and arised two lengths of 75 × 25mm softwood to 1,220mm, fix them in position at the back of the stringers using screws and glue. Starting from the bottom riser, fix all of the ris-

ers in position using screws and glue. This procedure will hold the structure in position, ready for the fixing of the treads. It is extremely important to ensure that the ends of the treads and risers run absolutely flush with the outside edges of the stringers, as failure to do so will result in the get-offs running out of square.

With the get-off treads now complete, all that remains is to dress the structure up by sanding and tidying up all edges. As a stock item of the theatre, it is a good idea to pay particular attention to the finish of these treads, as they will be called into use many times.

For a truly professional finish, a couple of modifications can be incorporated into the construction. The first improves the health and safety of the structure. Anyone who has tried to lift a sheet of 18mm ply will testify to the weight involved. It is a dense material that requires two people to lift safely. Bearing in mind that in excess of a whole sheet is used in this simple set of get-offs, it does not take a huge leap to realize that they will be a rather cumbersome structure. To alleviate this problem, remove the central area of the stringer material. Do this by marking a 75mm border along the back and bottom edges, allow a similar distance along the line of the treads forming a right-angled triangle. For neatness and ease of cutting, round off the corners by tracing

A standard set of get-off treads.

around a suitable circle such as a glue bottle or paint tin. Remove the marked area using a jigsaw and, observing good working practice, aris all edges. An indication of the sort of shape to work to is shown in the photograph.

Acoustical Modifications

A modification that can be applied to all treads and rostra is used when noise is an issue. Footfall on timber can be a noisy thing capable of disrupting the natural drama and flow of a scene. No audience wants to be distracted from the intimacy of hearing Hamlet deciding whether 'to be or not to be' by the clumping exit of Claudius and Polonius. The simple solution is to add a soft covering to the floor area. If a carpet is not appropriate to the set design, then the following method will solve the problem equally well.

Cut a strip of 4mm plywood 50mm in width and run it around the outside edges of each tread, fixing it in place using glue and flat-head nails or narrow-mouth staples. The space that is left in the middle of each tread should be covered with underfelt, glued and stapled in position. Finally, cover the entire tread with canvas and glue and staple again. After painting, the canvas will adhere to the underfelt creating a safe noise-deadening surface.

This method of tread construction will cover virtually all theatrical requirements encountered by the scenic carpenter. With the addition of handrails, mouldings or panelling, the get-off tread can become a realistic period staircase or a modern industrial focal point. The following section will cover these areas in brief, showing the basic methods that can be applied to a variety of different applications.

THE HANDRAIL AND NEWEL POST

The diagram below shows two methods of applying a handrail to a set of treads. To the bottom right is a suitable method for get-off treads; note the simple but effective collapsing system that will fold flat when not in use but still provide a rigid support. The handrail to the bottom left is more architectural, with a substantial newel post and spindles. The handrail is rebated underneath to receive the spindles and the uprights have all been housed into the treads to create rigidity and a sense of solid construction. It is a good idea to house the handrail into the newel post, as it will provide greater strength. These details are all highlighted in the diagram.

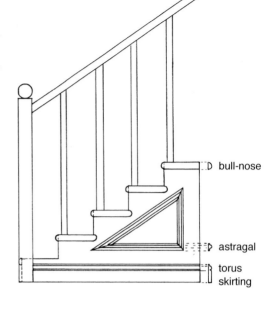

bull-nose

astragal

torus
skirting

NOSINGS AND MOULDINGS

To really flesh out a set of treads, a variety of mouldings can be fixed to them to give a more

Moulding and bull-nose have been added to create a more finished and decorative look.

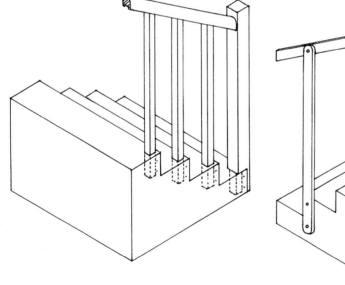

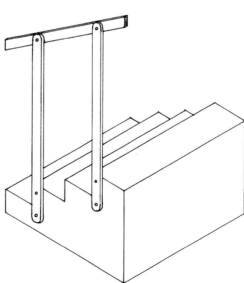

Two methods of fitting handrails.

architecturally accurate finish. Very few staircases in real life are built in the style already described above, however by adding a bull-nose moulding to the front edge or a decorative moulding such as torus or astragal (two easily available mouldings), the treads instantly become more interesting. The diagram (left) shows a variety of mouldings fitted in such a way as to create a more solid finish. Take care to glue all mouldings in position and, wherever possible, set the bull-nose slightly below the level of the tread to prevent them being kicked off when in use. Take note of the simple addition to the sides of the treads of panel moulding to create a more ornate finish simply by breaking up the lines of the treads.

DOGLEG-TREAD CONSTRUCTION

When space does not allow for the total number of treads required in a single run, it might be possible to break the run with a landing. The diagram below shows a simple method of creating the impression of a dogleg staircase by using a rostrum upon which to sit the upper

level of treads, as well as providing the landing up to which the lower treads can run. The advantage of constructing the treads in this manner is its portable nature. With three individual components, it makes for an easily movable structure without losing strength. By masking off the rostrum framework the illusion of solidity is created.

OPEN/LADDER-TREAD CONSTRUCTION

The other main style of tread encompasses a totally different construction method. The open or ladder method involves far more detailed construction and places greater demands on the budget, as the materials involved tend to be more expensive. The construction comprises two supporting lengths of timber, called stringers, that run diagonally from the bottom to the top of the run. In between the stringers are housed planks of timber called 'treads'. The treads are housed into the stringers with an additional supporting block underneath. The reasons for using this particular method may be for stylistic or

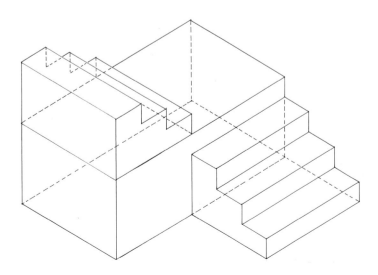

Diagram of dogleg treads.

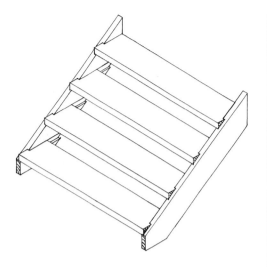

Tread Material Sizes

The following is a guide to the thickness of material recommended for various width treads.

1–450mm span: 25mm PAR (22mm)
450–600mm span: 32mm PAR (28mm)
600–1,000mm span: 38mm PAR (32mm)
1,000–1,220mm span: 50mm PAR (45mm).
The measurement in brackets is the finished or actual thickness after planing.

It is important to bear in mind that this is an approximate guide that will vary depending on a variety of factors including usage of treads, number of people using treads at one time and nature of usage.

(Above) Ladder construction treads.
(Below) A set of ladder treads used for a substage exit.

aesthetic reasons, or it may be called upon when the height to be reached is too great using block construction.

Because the treads have no support from underneath, it is necessary to use thicker timber to compensate.

Exactly the same method is used to arrive at the riser and going distances as was used in the solid tread example; however, that is where the similarities end.

CONSTRUCTING THE TREADS

Depending on the span and angle that the treads are required to cover, the width of the stringer will vary considerably. For a short, steep angle, a narrow width, say 100mm, may suffice; however, this would tend to be more appropriate for pitches of 60 degrees.

For pitches between 30 degrees and 45 degrees, a width of between 150mm and 200mm will be more suitable. The important factors are to maintain the depth of the tread –

an under-sized tread is dangerous and unacceptable – and to provide adequate support for it through the stringer material. If in doubt, follow this procedure: on a full sheet of ply or hardboard, mark-out the run of the treads; having referred to the thickness guide, try to be as accurate as possible showing the true size of the timber; now draw two lines, one touching the bottom, rear corner of each tread and the other running through the bottom, front corner of the treads. This will clearly show the required width of the stringer.

Try to work to standard sizes of material. Check with trade tables for the nearest comparable-sized timber, making sure that the finished size is taken into account.

Working on the construction of a similar set of treads to the solid set already covered, the stringers will be 150mm wide by 32mm thick. With an overall span of 1,220mm, the treads will be 250mm wide by 50mm thick. Now mark-out the treads themselves on to the stringers. Stringers come in pairs and it is important to remember this when marking-out. It is advisable to mark one stringer out first and then the second stringer off it. Using a piece of 4mm or 6mm ply, measure from one corner the distance of the riser and the depth of the tread in the other direction. This will act as a useful marking gauge. To make it even more useful, join the two marks up using a length of 25 × 25mm softwood, and do the same on the other side, thus creating a guide or fence to rest against the edge of the stringer.

The Mark-Out

Allow plenty of offcut, say 300mm; start by placing the gauge on the edge of the timber and marking along the riser and tread lines. This will create a triangle on the stringer that should be repeated to suit the number of treads required (in this case four). With this part of the mark-out complete, carefully measure the thickness of the tread material and mark it on

Marking Gauges

The marking gauge is a tool that requires practice to master: hold it like the handle-bar of a bicycle with thumb and forefinger on the fence block and the other three fingers holding the stem. To make a mark, hold the fence block firmly against the edge of the timber and drag the gauge with the pin facing away from the direction of travel. The aim is to leave a straight indelible line, so use it sparingly as it is a tedious job removing unwanted marks. When marking stringers, try to mark only where the actual tread will be.

to the stringer, so that it runs directly under the tread line. This will form parallel lines that form the housing for the tread. Form the housing by setting a marking gauge to 15mm and scribing a depth mark along the edges of the stringer. With a square, join the marks on the face of the timber to the scribed depth. This provides a clear indication of the waste material, which can now be removed.

There are a variety of methods that can be used to cut out the tread housings. One is to saw along the limit lines and remove the waste timber with a chisel. If this method is used, make sure to work in from both sides to avoid breakout of the timber. Alternatively, use a circular saw to cut out the bulk of the housing and clean the waste out, once again using a chisel.

If a router is available, the preferred method is to set up a jig and remove the waste using a flat-bottomed trenching bit. The jig consists of two pieces of timber that run across the stringer on the same angle as the treads. This will provide a guide to rout out the tread accurately every time, although of course it will need to be remade for different angled treads. Remember to work as accurately as possible.

The jig can be held in position when in use with temporary screws and simply slid up the stringer to each respective tread.

With this task complete, the bulk of the difficult work is done. To assemble the treads, first cut off the stringers to their correct length, removing the wastage that was allowed prior to set-out.

To cut the treads to correct length, simply measure the distance from the bottom of the tread housing to the outside edge of the stringer and multiply this by two. Subtract this amount from the overall width of the treads, which will leave the actual length of the individual treads. Cut them to size either with a panel saw, circular saw or ideally, if available, a radial-arm saw.

Set up on a bench with one of the stringers sitting on its edge, next offer up one of the treads to test for fit. If it is snug, glue using a suitable wood adhesive and fix in place using 75mm screws. Fit the other stringer to the other end and repeat this process for the other treads until all are fitted and fixed in position.

The danger with long runs of treads is separation of the structure under load. To combat this, fit a length of threaded rod across the width of the treads and bolt in position. Ideally the rod should run directly underneath the bottom, middle and top treads of a run. With washers and nuts fitted on either end, this will form a strong structure with far less tendency to spread.

These two methods of tread construction can be modified and adapted to suit virtually any requirement. With the incorporation of a suitable rostrum, a dogleg staircase can be easily constructed. To complete the effect, add suitable panelling to the exposed faces and dress with skirting and panel moulding.

SPACE-SAVING TREADS

Very often in smaller theatre spaces, little room is available in the wings for get-off treads. Often multi-level sets require the actor to exit from great heights but without the room to do so! The solution to this problem lies in staggered treads. This ingenious design vastly reduces the overall run required to achieve the same level of rise. Simply put, the staggered treads are comprised of two narrow sets of treads with double-height risers. When fixed side by side they form a set of treads that require the user to set off on a certain foot to enable them to climb efficiently. The diagram below shows a typical set of staggered get-offs and could be used wherever space is tight (and is it not so everywhere in the theatre?). In this example, climb the staircase by setting off on the left foot. Adjust the dimensions to suit each different situation.

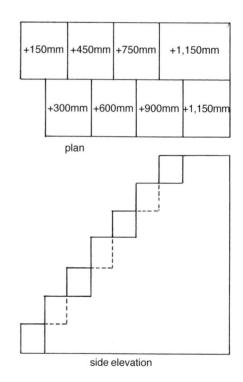

Space-saving staggered get-offs.

8 ROSTRUM AND TRUCK CONSTRUCTION

The construction of a basic gate-leg rostrum, including the joints, hinging and bracing, will be covered. Also the use and application of a modular steel rostrum and staging. In addition, basic truck construction will be covered, including the materials, wheels and brakes used, and the difference between fixed and swivel castors, as well as the use of different braking methods.

A rostrum is a raised area of staging used to create variety, height and form within a stage set. It can be as small as a block or as large as an entire stage, and can provide a bower for Titania to rest upon or an atmospheric battlefield for the Trojan army to advance upon. Whether Tosca is hurling herself from the top of the castle ramparts or PT Barnum is trying to fill his American Museum with the aid of a soapbox, they all have in common the fact that these pieces of scenery are different-sized rostra. A truck is a similar item of scenery with a significant difference: being mounted on castors, it is capable of moving on and off stage quickly and quietly.

HEALTH AND SAFETY AROUND ROSTRA AND TRUCKS

Rostra can be constructed in a variety of methods, the simplest being by forming 18mm plywood into a five-sided box, using much the same method as set out for solid treads in Chapter 7. Another type is the gate-leg rostrum, which is constructed in a similar fashion to the standard flat. However, the most important thing to remember when constructing any rostrum in any situation is safety. Bearing this in mind, it is vital to consider a few factors every time a rostrum is installed into a theatre.

* Ensure that the top is supported from underneath on all four sides. Failure to do this will result in sag, lack of strength and, the worst case scenario, collapse.
* How high is the rostrum? A risk assessment must be carried out whenever rostra or trucks are used on stage. The most common risk will be falling from the rostrum. It is up to each individual to rate the risk and address the potential appropriately. Handrails and kick boards can be incorporated to reduce the perceived risk and even pieces of furniture, such as bookcases and tables, can be used as a physical barrier to prevent the actor being put at risk. As has been said before, every set design is different and it is impossible in a book such as this to cater for every eventuality. Suffice to say, use your common sense and never put an actor at unnecessary risk through poor planning or negligence.
* Is an actor required to travel on the truck? Once again, use common sense and ingenuity to overcome the potential risk. Liaison with the director will help by arranging for

the actor to be sitting down or hanging onto a fixed piece of the structure while the truck is in motion. Ensure there are no overhanging structures, such as braces, etc., in the path of the truck that may impede the progress of the structure and, finally, ensure the stage area is clear of obstacles that may affect progress.

TYPES OF ROSTRA

The simplest method of rostrum construction is the block method. This uses 18mm ply to form an extremely sturdy construction that is quick to build. It can be made to virtually any size or shape, and is often used to form the base of a light truck construction. Being as solid as it is, it can prove to be extremely heavy to lift, so pay particular attention to removing as much of the surplus material as possible.

A standard 2,440 × 1,220mm rostrum might look something like the one in the diagram below. Notice that it is 200mm in height and has solid sides and intermediate supports.

This particular rostrum would be constructed from two sheets of 18mm ply. One of the sheets forms the top or lid of the rostrum and the other sheet is cut up to form the sides and

---

Weight-Saving Method

On any structure, such as trucks, rostra or treads, try to keep the weight down. This is best achieved by cutting the centre out of supporting walls, leaving a minimum of 75mm all around their outer edges. On long sides cut sections out leaving vertical supports every 600mm.

---

supports. The important thing to remember when making the cutting list is to subtract the thickness of the lid when cutting the sides, i.e. rather than cutting them at 200mm, cut them to 182mm. A slightly different adjustment must be made for the actual lengths of the sides. It will be easiest to use the full length of the sheet to form the long sides, meaning that it will be necessary to subtract twice the thickness of the ply to arrive at the actual length of the short sides. This being the case, the cutting list will look like this:

two lengths at 2,440 × 182mm
four lengths at 1,184 × 182mm.

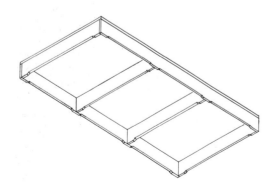

A typical solid rostrum shown from underneath.

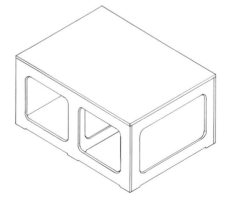

Weight-saving cut-out rostrum panels.

This cutting list allows for the two long sides, two short sides and two internal supports. These supports reduce spring in the rostrum and make for a stronger structure.

This principal can be applied to any block rostrum, but with higher structures it is a good idea to cut away any excess material from any unseen parts of the rostrum.

With all of the pieces cut out it is time to foot the bottom of the sides: this is done by cutting out a 15mm strip along the bottom edge of all the sides. Make sure to leave 100mm at each end and every 1,200mm in order to provide adequate support to the rostrum. This is done to prevent the rostrum rocking on uneven surfaces. Next fix the sides together with screws and glue, and fit the top. Having also fixed the internal supports in place, pre-mark their position on the top prior to fixing. Once again, fix the top in position with screws and glue.

BASIC TRUCK CONSTRUCTION

As well as making a rostrum, we have also managed to make a basic truck at the same time. As mentioned earlier in the chapter, a truck is simply a rostrum on wheels and this particular rostrum could be easily 'trucked' by fixing wheels or castors to its underside. To do this it is necessary to establish the load that is to be placed on the truck. Will it be required to carry furniture? How many actors will be on it at any one time? After establishing this, simply refer to the manufacturer's manual for your selected castor. As a rule, each type of castor will be rated to a certain weight or safe working load (SWL). However, as a truck of this size would require at least four castors, it is possible to multiply this weight by four to arrive at the size required. This is just the beginning, as you will find that there is a huge range of castors available on the market –

A truck brake in position. Hobson's Choice, RADA, Director Ellis Jones, *designer Alexander McPherson.*

certainly too many to go in this book. However, it is useful to establish a few factors before making the selection.

Firstly and obviously the weight is extremely important. Most problems with trucks occur because the selected castors are not strong enough for the job.

Secondly, it is necessary to take into account the noise factor. Nylon wheels are cheap but do sound like they are being driven over corrugated iron! Rubber wheels are quiet but more expensive.

Finally, are fixed, swivel or a mixture of both sorts of castors required? Using all swivel castors will make for a highly manoeuvrable but unstable truck, with the added difficulty of being hard to brake. Using all fixed wheels will make a truck that will only travel in straight lines. The best solution, as a rule, is to have a pair of swivel castors at one end and a pair of fixed castors at the other. By steering from the swivel end the truck becomes highly manoeuvrable, yet can be securely braked as well.

Truck Brakes

There are many patented truck brakes on the market, however they do tend to eat into a construction budget. One simple and cheap solution is to use a drop bolt into a hole in the stage floor. Make sure that it is permissible to drill into the floor before pursuing this option and also remember to allow plenty of time in the technical rehearsal for locating the holes effectively!

Other Braking Methods

In addition to the drop-bolt method of braking, it is worth considering two other methods in regular use in theatre today. Many castors are sold with a built-in foot-brake. These are ideal when there is ample access to the underside of the truck, as they can be locked in position using the operator's foot and released with a kick. Unless they are fitted with a locking swivel plate as well, there is a tendency for them to rotate slightly under stress, so have care in application.

The other braking method to be considered is an elevator brake. These devices fit on the back of a truck and physically lift the wheels off the ground, thereby immobilizing the truck. Once again, these should be fitted in conjunction with a combination of swivel castors on the rear of the truck and fixed castors on the front. Whilst these brakes are by far the most expensive method of truck immobilization, they are also the most effective. Bear in mind that they are re-usable and, once bought, will be used on trucks for years to come.

Finally, many modern trucks are run by electric motors that have built-in brakes. These are capable of running on tracks or freely over the stage area. Whilst most commonly used at the bigger-budget end of the industry, they are not out of the question for the smaller production and can be fitted to almost any sized truck.

Modular Steel Rostra

As with so much of scenic construction over the past couple of decades, the introduction of steel fabrication has meant a massive change in the way that effects are achieved. Flats are built of steel, as are ramps and treads, so perhaps it is not surprising that the rostrum is also now, most commonly, built of steel. In fact, the advent of the modular steel rostrum has revolutionized the theatre industry. As a rule, it is fitted with corner sockets that can take any length leg, therefore making them completely versatile. In addition, they are constructed in all of the most useful dimensions.

The other major advantage of steel rostra is the high strength factor relating to steel in this application. Many rostra are tested and rated to a specific SWL, making it easy to assess their usefulness. Being highly durable, steel rostra

Modular Rostrum Sizes

2,440 × 1,220mm (8 × 4ft)
1,220 × 1,220mm (4 × 4ft)
2,440 × 610mm (8 × 2ft)
1,830 × 1,220mm (6 × 4ft)
1,220 × 610mm (4 × 2ft)
2,440 × 1,220mm right-hand triangle
2,440 × 1,220mm left-hand triangle
These dimensions are a general indication of what is available and very often other shapes are freely available, such as quadrants and other curved pieces useful for the construction of a revolving stage.

also enjoy particularly long lives, making them very economical, as the only potential for damage is in the rostrum top itself. Bearing in mind the high cost of buying steel rostra, it is advisable to hire them instead. As well as saving money, the problem of post-show storage is also avoided.

GATE-LEG ROSTRA

Historically, every theatre owned a set of gate-leg rostra that would be used over and over again. As we have already seen, with the popular trend toward steel rostra, the wooden variety is a dying breed. It does have its uses, however, and deserves a brief mention at this time.

Gate-leg rostra are constructed from either 25 × 75mm or 32 × 75 mm softwood, and built in much the same fashion as a standard timber flat. Each rostrum is made from a number of 'flats' that hinge together to form a support structure for the top or lid of the rostra. The name comes from the appearance of the rostra, which, when constructed, looks like a series of old-fashioned garden gates.

The mortises are formed into the legs, the rails fit into the legs, with corner tenons at the top and mid-span tenons on the lower rail. Upright toggle-rails should be placed every 600mm to 800mm along the length of each frame and screwed into position.

One of the great advantages of this style of rostrum is its ability to fold away compactly. It

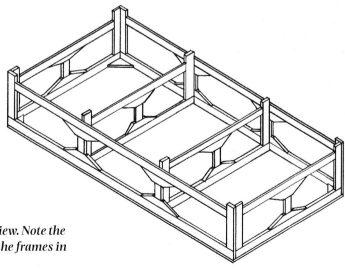

Gate-leg rostrum, underside view. Note the corner blocks in place to hold the frames in position on the rostrum lid.

is critical, however, to hinge the frames together accurately so as to ensure that they fold away correctly.

Assess the load incurred by the rostrum prior to construction. If it is likely to be required to withstand high loads, it may be advisable to increase the number of supports or gates used in each rostrum. As a rule it is a good idea to allow one internal gate for every 600–800mm. Allow for bracing to the frames when the height of the rostrum exceeds 600mm. With the rostrum frame constructed, sit the top on it and mark with a pencil the internal positions of the corners of the frame.

Turn the top over and fix a triangular corner block in position. These blocks will hold the top in place, as well as ensuring that the frame is square. Once the top is fitted correctly, it will be necessary to fix it down to the frame with screws, making it possible to be removed quickly and easily.

Trucking Gate-Leg Rostra

The easiest way to convert a gate-leg rostrum into a truck is to build a low-level truck as outlined earlier in the chapter and set the gate-leg on top. The rostrum can be fixed in place using pin hinges or locating blocks.

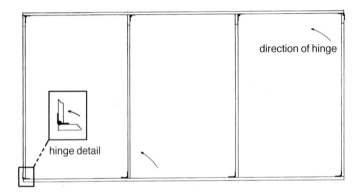

direction of hinge

hinge detail

Hinging arrangements of gate-leg rostrum.

Gate-leg on truck. A Midsummer Night's Dream, ROH. Note the diagonal bracing being used to stabilize the structure.

9 USEFUL JIGS AND THEIR APPLICATIONS

The jigs covered include: toggle-shoe jig, peg jig, radius jig, flat brace jig, scarf-joint jig, corner-block jig, ellipse jig and haunch jig (stencil).

With so many areas of scenic construction involving repetitive tasks, it is hardly surprising that the use of jigs in the workshop is as common as it is. By explanation, a jig, in this instance, is not the small dance that accompanies hitting one's thumb with a hammer. More usefully, it is a device that, when used in conjunction with another tool or machine, allows the scenic carpenter to complete these repetitive tasks quickly, efficiently and safely, in the knowledge that each work-piece will be an exact replica.

Pegs, braces and toggle shoes for flat construction, planking for floors and curves for reveals, all require mass production whilst maintaining an accurate finish. In any scenic workshop there will be evidence of tools, usually handmade, that are incorporated in the manufacture of these items. In this chapter, the basic as well as more advanced jigs will be covered, with an explanation of how they are used. All jigs only work when used in conjunction with another machine. To make this chapter as useful as possible, the tool or machine required is listed in brackets with the jig.

TOGGLE SHOE (TABLE OR TILT ARBOR SAW)

Make a master copy of a toggle shoe to use as a model: it should be 450mm long. Mark it out as in the diagram overleaf and cut off the waste. On a piece of 18mm ply, approximately 600 × 450mm, place the toggle shoe so that it projects over the left-hand edge by 20mm and trace around the outside edge. Cut out the waste, using either a jigsaw or band saw, and remember to aris all edges. The ply should be as large as is practical to increase safety. Ideally, there should be at least 300mm between the edge of the toggle shoe and the opposite edge of the ply. To aid grip when in use, fix a handle on to the top of the ply.

With the jig ready to use, place it on the saw bed and adjust the fence to suit. Place the first length of timber into the jig and pass it through the saw. Turn the timber around and remove

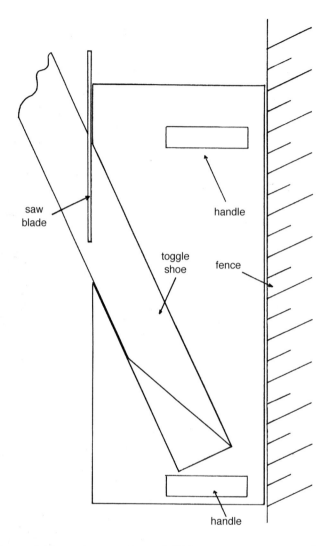

A toggle-shoe jig showing handles and position in relation to saw blade and fence.

saw blade

handle

toggle shoe

fence

handle

the angle from the opposite end. This process will produce a perfect replica of the original. By placing the offcut into the jig, it is possible to create another and so on.

By doing this, it is possible to create toggle shoes very quickly.

Peg/Wedge Jig (Band Saw)

To construct a flat, or indeed anything that involves mortise and tenon construction, a great number of wooden pegs are required. A simple jig that will see the end to endless whittling of matchsticks can be made from a small piece of 12mm or 18mm ply.

Referring to the diagram on page 86, cut out a piece of ply and mark out the notch shown on the right-hand side. Notice that plenty of room is allowed between where the blade will be cutting and the outside edge of the jig. To put this simple gadget into use place it on the bed of the band saw and adjust the fitted fence to provide a

84

(Above) Toggle-shoe jig in position on band saw.
(Below) Peg jig in position on band saw.

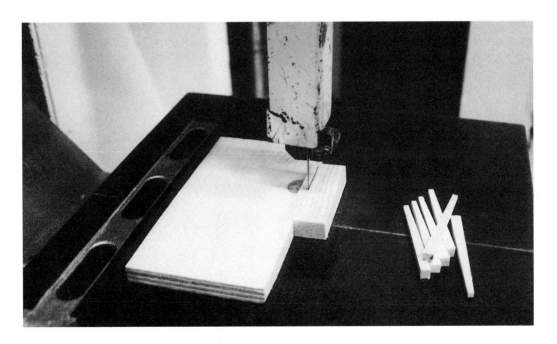

Peg-Cutting Made Easy!

Hook a bucket onto the bed of the band saw to act as a receptacle for the pegs. It is worth creating as many pegs as possible at one time, as they are always in demand. As with the toggle shoes, any offcuts in excess of 150mm in length should be kept in a box for recycling when time allows. The cutting of pegs and other stock items should always be done at quiet times to save valuable build time.

guide to the left-hand side of the jig. Place an off-cut of softwood into the notch and pass it through the saw. This creates a useful wedge that can be used in a variety of applications, particularly in tread construction. This is only the first of two steps. Turn the wedge on its side and place it back in the jig. By passing it through the saw a second time it is possible to create a tapered peg that is ideal for use in mortise and tenon construction. For mass production, run the softwood through the blade turning it end over end after each cut for maximum economy.

FLAT BRACE JIG (TABLE OR TILT ARBOR SAW)

When covering flattage with any soft material such as canvas or wool serge, it is important to provide diagonal bracing. These braces can be cut on a simple jig that is used on a table saw.

Working from the photograph (right), cut a piece of 18mm ply to match and cut a 45-degree notch into it. This will provide a good location for the timber whilst cutting it to equal lengths.

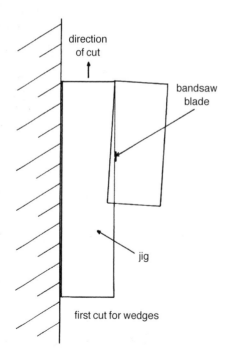

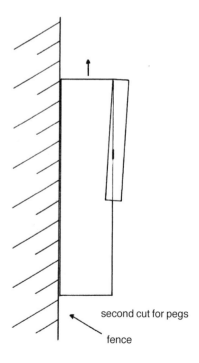

A peg jig showing its relation to the fence and blade.

The longest length will be ideal for large flat braces, however, when in need of shorter braces, it is not necessary to make a whole new jig: simply fix an insert in position with a hinge.

Brace-Cutting Tips

For a truly professional jig, fix a series of graded blocks in position by means of hinges every 100mm. This will provide the appropriate brace for any length required. All of the jigs mentioned so far should be constructed as securely as possible as they will be in use for many years. From a health and safety point of view it is vital to observe the most rigorous of construction processes, i.e. glue all joints, aris all edges and allow for plenty of clearance near the blade.

HAUNCH JIG

Whilst not necessarily a jig, as it does not enhance the use of another machine, a haunch jig is useful to have in the tool kit, as well as being easy to make. When constructing a lot of flats, the tedious job of marking out the tenon haunches on the stiles can be made simpler by using a stock outline. Take a piece of thin plywood, hardboard or even a piece of clear acrylic sheet, and cut it out to the shape of a corner tenon. Remember that the haunch is usually 25mm in width and 15mm in depth. By placing this jig on the uncut tenon, it is a simple matter to trace around the outside, the result being a perfect mark-out every time. It can also be used to mark out the haunch on the corner mortise by placing it in position on top

A simple brace jig.

of the limit lines and marking accurately with a sharp pencil.

Apart from these common jigs, it is possible to look at a number of other useful jigs and gadgets that will come in handy in any workshop.

As a famous Italian artist once said, the most difficult thing to make is a perfect circle, and it is certainly not easy to cut one in timber, even with the sharpest of tools, but with a simple guide, a router will become an ideal cutting compass, just as another device will cut a perfect ellipse. The next two jigs will require a moderate amount of time in construction, however the end result is worth it.

ROUTING COMPASS (ROUTER)

A length of 20 × 5mm metal bar is needed to construct this jig, along with a small amount of metal dowel to suit. Cut the bar to 1,000mm in length and drill a series of 5mm holes along it at 25mm intervals. Another short length of the bar should be bent to match the outer shape of the router and cut to length. Weld the two pieces of metal together into a T shape. Mark the position of the guide holes on to the top of the T and weld the dowel in these positions. The dowels should be able to slide into the router's guide holes, being held in position by means of the locking screws. This gadget will

cut a perfect circle at any radius required. For radii less than 1,000mm, simply locate the appropriate hole over the centre point and adjust the router cutter to suit. For a longer radius, fix a length of timber onto the top of the compass T and measure out the required distance

For clarification, look at the accompanying diagram and photograph below. This jig will prove invaluable for window, door or table construction and can be easily carried in a basic tool kit.

The router compass in use.

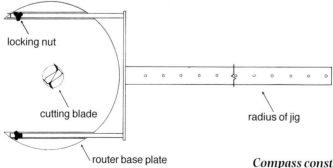

locking nut

cutting blade

radius of jig

router base plate

Compass construction in relation to the router.

ELLIPSE JIG (ROUTER)

Another useful jig can be simply made for cutting a perfect ellipse. An ellipse is a regular oval formed by tracing a curve following a long and short axis. The necessary jig should be made as per the diagram below showing all construction details.

With the body of the jig constructed, it is necessary to fit a length of metal dowel to the jig. As for the compass, the dowel should fit into the guide holes of the router, so that it can be secured firmly in place. Drill a series of 3.5mm holes along the length of the dowel (the closer the holes are together, the better). To cut the ellipse, locate the jig in the dead centre of the ellipse to be cut. Place the router in position for the longer axis. Fit the dowel to the jig block by means of a panel pin on the A axis. Now place the router in position for the short axis and fit the second block in position on axis B in the same manner. Double-check the position of the router on both axes and commence the cutting process.

When cutting a larger sized ellipse, it may be easier to use a second pair of hands to ensure the pins stay in position during operation. Slippage of the router could result in a miss-cut that leads to wastage of materials and time. It is good health and safety practice to have a co-worker in attendance whenever you are using a power tool, particularly when new to the process.

As with the compass jig, this gadget will cut up to any length that can be accommodated by the dowel. Bulkheads, windows and doors can all be cut using this method, making a potentially tricky task easy.

Two jigs that are used occasionally in the scenic workshop are the corner-block jig and scarfe-joint jig. The corner-block jig is used to construct triangular strengthening blocks for staircase construction, as well as any area where a right-angled joint requires additional strength. Examples of this are in block-rostrum construction or truck construction.

The scarfe-joint jig is used as a means to extend timber in length when a straight, clean line is necessary, such as in flat construction. The longest length available from most timber yards is 6,000mm, so when longer lengths are required, this joint is invaluable.

CORNER-BLOCK JIG (BAND SAW)

To cut corner blocks would normally require an adjustment to the band-saw table to 45 degrees each time a block was required. This can take valuable time, as well as not always producing a satisfactory result. Using a jig will

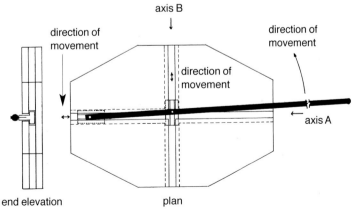

Construction of ellipse jig. end elevation plan

provide a superior method of production in a more efficient manner.

To make the jig, cut a piece of 18mm ply to the size of the band-saw table and carefully run it through the blade so that it sits on, and covers, the table with the blade projecting from the middle. Using a combination square, run a line from the blade to the edge of the timber in front of, and behind, the blade. Set the table to 45 degrees (this will be the only time that it will be necessary to do this) and saw a length of 50 × 50mm PAR softwood the length of the table diagonally along its length. Using the two triangular pieces of timber that have been created by doing this, glue and screw them longest side down on either side of the line. This provides an ideal support when cutting any timber to 45 degrees. For added safety and efficiency, fix a length of timber along the front edge of the jig to stop it sliding over the table when in use.

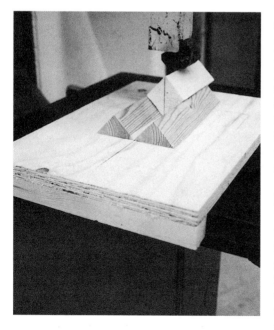

Corner-block jig.

SCARFE-JOINT JIG (RIP SAW, DIMENSION SAW, TABLE SAW)

Timber can be joined along its length by simply fixing a splint to both pieces of timber and screwing and gluing it together, but this is an unsightly process that will create a joint that is twice the thickness of the rest of the timber. To solve this problem, a professional scenic carpenter incorporates a scarfe joint. This joint consists of two long, angled cuts, one on the end of each piece of timber to be joined, that when joined together form a strong, slimline bond that is ideal when constructing flattage or any other set piece. The jig required to do this is by far the longest standard jig in the workshop. To make it, take a length of 18mm ply approximately 610mm in width and 2,000mm in length. Cut one length of the sheet to a 5-degree angle. Usually, the fitted fence of a table saw runs on the right-hand side of the blade. If this is the case, make the cut on the left-hand side of the ply. Now fix a length of 75 × 25mm PAR softwood all the way along the length of the angled cut. This will act as an invaluable aid to holding the timber in place during the cutting process. It is best to clamp the timber to be cut so that it projects slightly out the front of the jig. Set the fence on the saw so that the blade is in the correct position and begin the cut. Complete the joint by gluing and nailing the two ends together. Use 38mm flathead nails and bend the exposed ends over to lock the joint together.

Health and Safety

When cutting through any timber, it is important not to force the material – it is especially important to bear this in mind when cutting a scarfe joint. The timber is being cut on edge, therein creating potential balance problems as well as the fact that many saws will be near to their maximum cutting capacity when sawing through 70mm of thickness. Take it slowly and the result will prove more satisfactory.

10 SCENIC-PAINTING INTERPRETATION AND SAMPLING

This chapter will cover the model-showing, where all relevant information concerning the set is discussed, such as the materials to be used and what paint effects and finishes are required. Scenic interpretation of the design is explained, through to the making up of samples and use of references for this purpose.

Before a set has been painted, a scaled-up sample of the finished effect is often required for two reasons. First, to give the designer an idea of how the final painted effect will be, and, second, to give the scenic artist a valuable chance to work out exactly which processes will be used in order to create the desired effect. This chapter covers this essential process, from the scenic interpretation of the design, to the making up of these sample pieces and relevant, and important, use of references for the scenic artist.

UNDERSTANDING SCENIC INTERPRETATION

It is important to mention the key role of *interpretation* within scenic art. The scenic artist's role is very much that of an *interpreter* rather than a *copyist*, as some people would inaccurately describe. It is their job to convey the spirit of a design in a safe and practical way, up to twenty-five times larger than the given model. Historically this was not the case, as the designer was more often than not a scenic artist as well, and therefore painted his or her own sets. Times have changed, and it was in the latter half of the twentieth century that we saw the emergence of scenic *artist*, as well as *theatre designer*, as two quite different careers.

There are of course exceptions, as some designers like to paint, and some scenic artists also design. A designer will occasionally work alongside a scenic artist on their own set, and this can be enjoyable as ideas and skills are shared. Generally speaking, however, most scenic artists prefer to be left well alone to get on with their side of the artistic process, with critical intervention only where necessary; the two careers are quite separate, requiring both levels of skill in equal measures to obtain successful results.

To be able to interpret a design well, one of the most important skills is communication, both with the designer and the rest of the production team, especially if the production processes are to run smoothly and successfully. There are bound to be certain hurdles to cross as the work progresses, but the better the communication is from the start, the easier it will be to sort these out. The scenic artist must be able to discuss their work from the very beginning with the designer and, unlike some careers in art, such as fine art or illustration, this is a job where the scenic artist will be always working for somebody else's creative vision, and more often than not as part of a team. This is not the scenic artist's design, but it is the scenic artist's job to interpret it to the best of their ability, and to be able to convey this successfully in scenic terms. For the individual who wishes to either work alone or to paint entirely for his or herself, then this is not the right career for them. Some people may feel that artistically one cannot get real satisfaction when working on someone else's creative ideas, but as the rest of this book will show, the skills and diversity of scenic art are hugely challenging and creative, which in turn is highly fulfilling.

LOOKING AT THE MODEL

At the first model-showing, the scenic artist meets the designer and sees the scale model for the very first time, either as a white-card model or as a finished painted design. The designer will normally give a brief description of the set, sometimes describing inspirations and ideas but, most importantly, their production requirements for the design. In the very early stages of any production the director will have decided how the overall concept of a production is going to be staged, and will have communicated these ideas to the designer whose job it is to convey this visually by the design, for example, whether or not a production is to be set in modern day or in period.

As the model is looked at, the scenic artist will have begun to formulate ideas of how to realize the final effect by way of talking to the designer, closely looking at the model and analysing what it is that they are actually seeing. During these early discussions, the scenic artist will be asking key questions, and offering their ideas and suggestions, so that decisions are made.

At this meeting, detailed discussions are extremely important. They have major budgetary implications that, as mentioned in the Chapter 1, are important to sort out from the beginning. Potential problems can be ironed out and it is up to the appropriate production staff to mention these now. For example, where there is a lot of time-consuming detailed paintwork on a set, and very little production time, this is the moment for the scenic artist to

1:25 scale model of **Shy Man at the Palace,** *designed by Roger Butlin.*

An Outline of the Kind of Questions to Ask

- What is the overall feel of the design? (There will be certain effects that even an experienced designer will have difficulties in expressing in a small-scale model and that can only be seen in full size, e.g. wood graining. A question like this helps the scenic artist understand more fully what it is that the designer wishes to convey to an audience, such as realism or expressionism.)
- How much is available in the budget? Cheaper alternatives may have to be used where too costly requirements are made.
- Where a brick texture is shown, are these to be two- or three-dimensional?
- What kind of materials has the designer in mind for flown cloths?
- If the floor has a marble effect, what kind of varnish is required? A high sheen or matt finish?
- If there are wooden floors, are they to be real or painted?
- If there is a texture, what level of realism is required?

As well as the more practical questions, such as:

- Will the performers be barefooted where a rough textured floor could be a potential health and safety issue?
- How many performances are there going to be, as this may alter decisions about certain costs? It would seem unwise spending a small fortune on an expensive varnish for a floor, when there are only three performances, and a cheaper alternative can be used that is as effective in the short term.

discuss this with the designer, to either adjust the designs or try to gain more production time through talking to the production manager.

Once these questions have been raised, a further meeting, to be held at a later date, is often arranged between the designer and other departments to discuss their individual requirements in more detail. At this point the scenic artist can start to prepare samples in advance of the next meeting.

THE USE OF REFERENCES IN SCENIC ART

Having received the model from the designer, there may well be other references given to the scenic artist as well. These would include such items as photographs, books, magazine cuttings, colour swatches, as well as actual pieces of stone, fabrics and many other miscellaneous

A Tip for Anyone Wishing to Study Scenic Art at a College

If you are hoping to study scenic art at a college, it is a really good idea to keep a scrapbook/sketch pad to record all your theatre work and relevant experiences, such as school productions, theatre and exhibitions, visits, etc., as well as any observations taken from life in general, as it will be useful to take to your interview along with your portfolio of artwork. By sketching and recording a variety of images taken from these experiences, an individual will be expressing their interest in the diversity needed to be a scenic artist. At this stage, no college expects a full portfolio of scenic work but such a scrapbook/diary shows that you are really interested in the subject.

items that have been used in the design process. These are all of great importance and must be treated with as much care as the model itself. They are at times items of great sentimental value too, such as the fragment of 1930s linoleum used as a reference, or the ornamental death mask from a designer's own garden.

These references will have been drawn from the designer's own collection or obtained through their research for a particular production. This brings us to the point of discussing

how important it is for the aspiring scenic artist to start compiling his or her own reference library, which will prove to be invaluable.

First, as so much of the scenic artist's role is about observation, it is a really good idea to keep a scrapbook or visual diary of your work as you progress. Many colleges that teach scenic art include this in their programme of work, as a way of recording the student's progress. Keeping such a diary is an interesting and useful method of recalling methods and processes,

A typical selection of references used by a scenic artist.

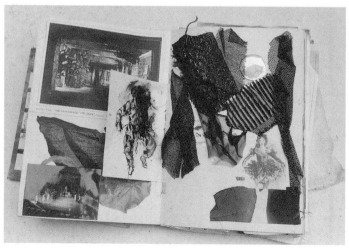

A scrapbook is an excellent way of recording work and relevant experiences.

even if you are not a student. For example, collect relevant photos, snippets of the actual materials used, working drawings, sample colours, postcards, photocopies and so on, the list is endless, but put together with a written diary of events, the diary will become your bible.

This book covers all the relevant basic techniques and methods required for the scenic artist; it is of great use to collect books and other references on appropriate subjects, such as architecture and life drawing, as well as a variety of other books to build up your own visual library. Understandably these are not cheap – especially glossy hardbacks – however, there are always good second-hand shops, as well as Christmas and birthday presents. A cheaper and good source of pictorial references is postcards, magazines and greetings cards. Images of nature, textures, people, places, etc., are all really useful to the scenic artist, and if you are handy with the camera, you can take photos of such images yourself too.

Other excellent references to have are manufacturers' sample cards for paints, scenic fabrics, dyes and so on. These can be used in meetings with designers as direct reference points, or for your own use when budgeting, mixing colours or simply painting. Finally, on the subject of references, there are the three-dimensional items to be considered, such as fragments of marble, stone, or bark. Books, photos and other pictorial references are extremely important, but in order to really understand, and therefore accurately interpret a form such as marble, there is nothing in the world that compares to analysing and studying the real item. Therefore, wherever possible, try to collect a sample of the particular object required.

PREPARING SAMPLES

In order to make samples, the scenic artist will have the scale model of the set or at least the appropriate pieces of it, as well as any other reference material the designer may have passed on.

There will always be the temptation to start painting a piece of scenery as soon as you can, as, quite understandably, painting or texturing can be a great pleasure. But in a job where time is precious, and mistakes difficult and at times costly to rectify on such a large scale, the process of sampling cannot be too highly recommended. Undoubtedly it will save time and money in the long run. For even the most

Reference books are vital to the scenic artist.

experienced scenic artist, certain designs can be challenging to interpret, and it is only by taking the time to accurately work out the processes by which an effect can be skilfully achieved, that they can confidently approach the real thing. It is better to be safe than sorry, as the saying goes.

The process of sampling can sometimes be more pleasurable than the job itself as, not unlike the research into an essay or art project, it is possible to freely experiment here, using hands and mind alike to work out the processes. Once a sample has been accepted by both designer and painter, it is an extremely important focal point to keep throughout the painting process, not only for yourself but, perhaps more importantly, for the rest of the team, when there is more than one scenic artist on the same job. Scenic effects have to look stylistically as *one*, and a sample will be kept as a guide for reference.

The sample is also useful when there is a great deal of repetition in a design over a number of pieces that cannot always be seen together for whatever reason (normally a lack of space). Here the sample is used as a constant reminder of exactly how the effect should be. In productions where there may be a number of painters involved in painting the set, the

(Inset) This shows a close-up of the sample of painting to scale (shown at 50 per cent actual size), to present to the designer.
(Main picture) The actual set piece.

Protecting the Model

In order to protect the model, as it will come under some extremely heavy fire over the various production processes, it is extremely wise to cover the individual sections with a protective layer of acetate (available from your local art suppliers). Where acetate is not available, or a cheaper alternative required, polythene or even clingfilm will do, but for accurate colour references, or drawing out, this must be removed beforehand for a clearer observation. This is also extremely useful for doing any drawing or measuring marks on to the model pieces, as it is not wise to mark the actual designs. In a highly professional capacity, certain models are worth a great deal of money, and it is good practice to start looking after them – quite apart from the fact that models are the work of someone else and should be treated with respect.

difficulty of keeping the styles as similar as possible is easy to imagine; the use of the sample is one way of helping to achieve this.

A sample needs to be a scaled-up example of the painted finish for a set. This could be a section of wood grain, brickwork or watercolour effect. It is wise to do a relatively simple section, as a complicated and elaborate example will be too confusing in such a small sample. A good size is around 1m², but often depends on the effect you are painting: a design that incorporates a large repeat pattern wallpaper design will look better on a larger piece. If you are doing a sample of painting for a cloth, it is important to do it on the same material as the cloth, as paint will react very differently on the many different scenic fabrics available. Otherwise use a scrap of hardboard, ply or whatever you have to spare in the workshop. The most important aspect of a sample is to treat it in exactly the same way from the start, as you will later treat the actual piece of scenery. That is to say, having sanded the surface to get a nice even finish, then primed and painted your

---

Example of Paint Recipe

Present Laughter floor parquet colours for wood-graining.

List of colours needed: prime, first colour glaze, second colour glaze, lining in colour for individual blocks, final varnish.

- Prime: mix of white emulsion, yellow ochre, raw sienna and raw umber.
- First colour glaze: 50/50 mix of satin and matt emulsion glaze, burnt umber, burnt sienna, water.
- Second colour glaze: 50/50 mix of satin and matt emulsion glaze, raw sienna.
- Lining in colour: glaze, black, burnt umber, and water.
- Final varnish: pacific one, satin finish.

---

effect, you can be assured that when the same procedures are later followed, the effects should be pretty much the same. One way of recording exactly which processes were used is to write them down, quite literally, as recipes; where colours are concerned, this is particularly useful. As particular colours are recorded, take a small sample of fabric or wood that has been prepared in the same way as the samples, and place a mark of colour to be used later as a direct reference. No matter how much you think you will be able to remember of a process or colour mix at a later date, do not trust this assumption. It is also a useful way of allowing others to follow these instructions, in the same way that a cook will utilize a recipe.

PRESENTING THE SAMPLE

If your sample has to be shown to a designer, it is a good idea to present it in a way that will simulate the actual stage situation as much as possible. For example, where a piece of scenery is going to be seen at a great distance on stage, then allow the designer to see the sample at a similar distance too. Or where a piece of scenery will only ever be seen under very low lighting, then try to simulate this as far as you can in your workshop space. All this will help both you and the designer to get a truer picture of what the rest of the set will look like when it is later painted. For some inexperienced designers, the process of seeing their work enlarged greatly can be a daunting one, and the more you can do to assure them, the easier your job will be too. If you gain a designer's confidence, half the battle is won and you will feel more confident too.

This use of writing down certain processes and formulas is also extremely handy when other scenic artists are required to use them for whatever reason, such as the absence of the painter who made a particular sample.

11 SURFACES

An explanation will be given of the many different materials used in theatre design that can have paint and textures applied to them, such as the traditional canvasses, gauze, silk and serge, through to the more recent PVCs, vinyl floorings and metallics. A short description is also given of the materials used by designers whose work reflects the trend in design today towards the use of greater realism in the true sense of the word. These can include any natural or man-made materials that may or may not have any paints or textures applied to them. An explanation of the laying down, putting up and stretching of such materials will be given, outlining the differences of floor- and frame-painting, as well giving an explanation of the correct preparation of these materials prior to the commencement of the painting process.

Theatre design has changed drastically from a hundred years ago, where 'realism' was expressed in the form of the great painted illusion, as seen by the work of masters such as Leon Bakst or Alexandre Benois. As Ronald Harwood says in *All the World's a Stage*, it was as if, 'all through this century as if by an unspoken agreement, the theatre was being prepared for change'. These changes in design were brought about by the work of designers such as Edward Gordon Craig and Adolphe Appia in Europe, and the director Vsevolod Meyerhold in Russia, whose revolutionary ideas were to bring about the birth of modernism in theatre design. To quote Harwood, 'Craig, like the playwrights, dispensed with realism and favoured a setting more symbolic of the play as a whole, and therefore bound to be more abstract'. This meant that for some designers, what was used on the stage as part

List Showing the Composition of Stage Scenery Exactly

- backcloth
- frontcloth
- sets of legs
- sets of borders
- cycloramas, otherwise known as a cyc
- cut cloths
- gauzes.

All of the above can be made up from a variety of different scenic materials:

- stage cloths are traditionally made from cotton duck canvas;
- flattage: all the walls or hard scenery are made up from a wooden or metal structure and traditionally covered in canvasses, or plywood, though they can also be covered in a choice of other materials, as listed;
- constructed scenery consists mainly of wooden or metal structures;
- stage flooring can be pretty much any material that has been safely treated for theatrical use, such as wood, vinyls, or the less traditional materials listed next;
- ground row is traditionally constructed from wood, metal and canvas.

of a design was no longer represented by just a painted illusion. In a design, the very essence of a shape, material or image, whether realistic or abstract, was to play just as an important a role. Today this has been taken even further, with the convergence of both technology in stage design, and 'realism' in the true sense of the word. The scenic artist can, therefore, expect to see diversity in designs ranging from the most abstract minimalist stage settings to the more traditional painted forms, and where photography, computer-aided design and photocopiers are now widely used in the design process. For the scenic artist this means two things: first, that they can expect to work on, and with, a number of radically new and exciting materials; and, second, that it makes the job more challenging, as interpreting and re-creating some of these images is not as straightforward as it seems in comparison to the more traditional painted sets.

Whether or not it is the arrival of these new materials that changed stage design, or whether the designs themselves necessitated a need for change, is a matter of interesting discussion. However, the fact remains that as stage design has developed and changed, then so have the materials and methods of scenic art. In this chapter, the wide variety of scenic materials used will be looked at, from the conventional timeless canvasses and gauzes, to the more recent and greatly effective materials such as PVCs, vinyls, metallics and plastics. Preparation of all these materials will be explained and a description given of both floor-painting, otherwise known as 'the continental' method, and frame-painting.

An example of a set that uses mainly traditional materials. RADA production of **Present Laughter,** *by Noel Coward. Designed by Peter Rice, directed by Robert Chetwyn.*

When designing a stage set, a designer will take into consideration the visual, tactile and sound qualities of the surfaces in relation to the design as a whole. A surface can conjure up a powerful effect on the imagination, such as metal being perceived as an unyielding strength, or flowing silks evocative to our sensual perceptions. This is an important aspect of any design, and the use of the right materials will help further the effect that a designer is trying to portray. Decisions about the exact materials to be used are normally finalized by the end of the sampling process at the very least, if not beforehand. A scenic artist will have an important part in these decisions, as often a design can reveal some interesting surface requirements that demand the experiences of a scenic artist in order to convey ideas and potential possibilities. Up to a century ago, the demands of the scenic artist would have been of a different nature, as designs were more about the painted illusion and sets were made up from soft cloths and flattage. Decisions then will have been more about the qualities and styles of painting, rather than the choices of materials. The role of a scenic artist has, therefore, altered as the history of design has developed. This is not to say that decisions such as these are not made today, but stage design, as described earlier, now embraces a far wider variety of materials.

Historically, most theatre designers followed a set formula for a design, whereas today there is far greater freedom. An audience may expect to see designs ranging from a stage devoid of all scenery, to a set created entirely from back projections, or a design consisting of an elaborate mixture of both conventional scenery with the more modern techniques and materials now available. To start with, traditional scenic materials will be considered. All these materials are available from specialist scenic suppliers listed at the end of the book. Canvasses can also be bought from most fine art suppliers, which are also listed.

TRADITIONAL FABRIC SCENIC MATERIALS

The following scenic materials are made from linen/flax, cotton, wool or silk.

Canvasses

These are available in a variety of cottons and flaxes, and were traditionally used due to the fact that they shrink when in contact with water. They come in a variety of weights, widths and qualities, and are at times bleached or unbleached. The choice of which to choose normally lies in the designs, the budget, the width sizes available or, at times, is the personal choice of the painter or designer. Canvasses are for use in the make-up of soft cloths, or for covering flattage. Matting duck or cotton duck canvasses are traditionally used for painting stage cloths, as they are particularly tough and durable.

Filled Cloth

These are sometimes referred to as a filled gauze. They are available in vast widths that, unlike most canvasses, do not require seams: this means that they can be backlit and require no priming.

Calicos and Sheeting

These are cotton lightweight materials, and are used in the make-up of cloths, as they come in a variety of widths and weights. They are a good cheap alternative for painting on if there is a tight budget, and are also useful for flattage: either stuck onto ply or stretched over a wood or metal frame.

Gauzes

These are mostly available in black, white or grey, and in varying widths. They range from the fine gauzes, to square, sharkstooth, scenic, bobbin, reflective and a number of others. The differences lie in the shape and size of holes,

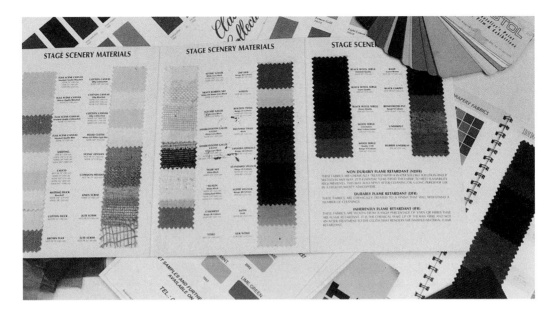

The many materials available are chosen from sample cards.

which have differing effects under lighting. The true effect of gauze is dependent entirely on stage lighting.

Muslin

Rarely used for made-up cloths, but is available in large widths, if required. However, its translucent nature makes it a useful fabric for use on stage, as well as in the paintshop, mainly as rags for painting.

Stage Velvet/Velours

These heavyweight fabrics are used for two purposes mainly: first, for sound absorption as masking; and, second, for painting on, as it creates a beautiful surface to absorb both paint and light.

Wool Serge

The properties of this are similar to that of stage velvet, and it is often used for masking flats but can also be painted on.

Chinese Silk/Jap Silk

These are available in a great variety of colours, but come in limited widths and are expensive. Cheaper alternatives are man-made products, but they are not quite as efficient as the inherent luxurious quality of silks.

Jutes/Hessians

These highly textural fabrics are available in different widths and qualities, and their uses vary from prop to scenic effects.

MODERN SCENIC MATERIALS

Apart from traditional fabrics, there is a wide range of exciting and highly effective stage materials available on the market. Many of the materials listed were not originally intended for scenic painting purposes! Experience has shown that they can be, and certainly are, used by designers and scenic artists as alternative surfaces.

101

PVC (Polyvinyl Chloride)

These came into existence in the mid-1960s, are available in various widths and can be made up into hanging cloths. Types such as Revue, Studio and Glassclear, are mainly used for front and rear projections on stage, but are also used in other entertainment businesses. They can also be used in the traditional scenic sense as a painted and textural surface.

Polyvinyl Metallics

These are made from PVC, polyesters, polystyrene and acetates, and are available in a variety of widths, weights, in flexible or semi-rigid forms. Variations are available such as: mirrors, mosaic mirrors, glitter cloths, transparent metallics and laser scrims. They are all used as both painted and non-painted surfaces.

A backcloth for La Ronde *by the Royal Ballet. Designer John McFarlane. This was painted on Revue, a PVC material traditionally used for back projections, as it fulfilled the designers' wishes to resemble tracing paper.*

The set for Junk, *directed by John Rettalack and designed by Niki Turner, uses simple unpainted black mirrored formica as flooring.*

Contra H

This is a highly textural material available in different weights and qualities, which is made from viscose.

Fibreglass/Woven Glass

Available in multi-colours, widths and varieties, and mainly used as a fire preventive, for example for placing behind lamps.

Arena 86

This is a PVC screen made up from many holes designed as a wind resister, as it is used for projections outdoors.

Synthetic Gauzes

Made from polyethylene mash, these are available in different sizes and in black and white. Ideal for front projections.

An example of how the use of a mirrored floor has created stunning visual effects, as seen here in The Rover *by Aphra Ben. Designed by Niki Turner and directed by Jonathan Church.*

This design, by Niki Turner for Further Than the Furthest Thing, *by Zinnie Harris and directed by Irina Brown for the RNT, uses Glassclear, mirrored formica, chipped rubber foam, back projection material and Idenden.*

Laser Gauzes

These are made from polyester and polyamides and are used in conjunction with lasers to create stunning effects.

TOWARDS GREATER REALISM

The final category of surfaces may be termed as miscellaneous. Recent years of theatre design have shown a move towards greater realism. For many designers the art of the painted illusion has taken a back seat, as often a real material is chosen in preference to a painted one, though obviously this can have a great effect on a budget, for example, the choice of a solid oak floor will be far more expensive than a painted one. Another problem is the impracticality of these materials: an oak floor is a lot heavier, which is highly inconvenient for touring shows. It remains to be seen whether or not this trend will continue. Here is a list of the type of materials used for such purposes:

* metals: such as bronze, aluminium, steel in solid or meshes;
* carpets and other interior floorings, such as linoleums;
* natural substances, such as soils, sands, stones, bricks, water and grass.

FLOOR- AND FRAME-PAINTING

Having looked at the three categories of surfaces, which a scenic artist may use as part of their work, it is now important to look at the two different methods of painting in scenic art,

An example of a set where realism is used in the literal sense with actual sand filling the floor space. **Things Fall Apart** *by Biyi Bandele, designer Niki Turner, director Chuck Mike.*

Fire-Proofing

All materials used to ensure realism need to be checked and treated with any relevant fire-retardants, as described, where needed.

All materials available from specialist scenic suppliers are treated with flame-retarders/fire-proofers, unless specifically required not to be. This is an extremely important issue, as all fire regulations must be strictly observed at all times. Specifications are as follows as quoted from J.D. McDougall Ltd (*see* Useful Addresses):

- NDFR (non-durably flame-retardant). These fabrics are chemically treated with a water-soluble solution. If wetted in any way, it is essential to retreat the fabric to meet flammability requirements. This may also apply after cleaning or a long period of use in a high humidity atmosphere.
- DFR (durably flame retardant). These fabrics are chemically treated to withstand a number of cleanings.
- IFR (inherently flame retardant). These fabrics are woven from a high percentage of yarn or fabrics that are flame-retardant. It is the chemical make-up of the raw fibre, and not an after treatment to the cloth, that renders the finished material flame-retardant.
- BS 5867 part 2 type B. All durably and inherently flame-retardant fabrics are produced to comply with the flammability requirements of BS 5867 part 2 type B: fabrics for curtains and drapes.

Occasionally, certain non-fire-proofed items on a set may require fire-proofing. This must be followed out with due care and attention, as the main component is sodium. This comes in a liquid or crystal form, and is usually applied from a garden sprayer or hand-pump sprayer. Protective clothing must be worn.

and the preparation of all such materials, where relevant.

There are two main techniques for painting scenery:

- ✳ **Frame-painting**. A scenic artist paints whilst standing in a vertical position either on a paint frame, a paint gantry or a paint bridge. Scenery, mostly in the form of soft cloths, is stretched onto a solid frame and thus enables the scenic artists to work on it from this position

Working on a frame.

✳ **Floor-painting**. Scenery is worked on, after it has been stretched out, or laid on, the floor. The scenic artists will either stand directly onto the surfaces, whilst using extended tools or, on occasions, squat, kneel or sit! This is known as the 'continental' method, having developed in Europe.

Each method of painting has its own characteristics and for the genuine enthusiast it is a good idea to become acquainted with both, as most professional scenic studios use both methods. A description is now given of the characteristics and techniques involved, and an example given for preparing a made-up canvas cloth using both methods; the differences will be pointed out, wherever necessary.

The Paint Frame

The main advantage of having a frame is the fact that it does not take up so much space, unlike the amount needed for floor-painting. It is also physically easier on the scenic artists as not nearly so much bending or kneeling is

Working on the floor.

A cloth being hung on a frame.

106

required. A slight disadvantage is that it can take longer to prepare your cloth for painting, as each process requires the movement of the frame regularly, as opposed to simply walking around. The methods of painting on a frame call for less splashing and freedom with wet paint, as any over-wetting will cause the paint to run and potentially ruin your cloth! A paint trolley is advisable to house all equipment, as well as acting as a palette for mixing colours.

Hazards to look out for include being careful not to push too hard while painting, as the frame itself will appear as the brush catches onto the wood behind. Also, on certain gantries and bridges, it is possible to drop tools and equipment down to floor level, if not enough care is taken.

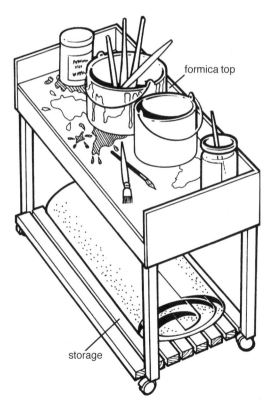

A typical paint trolley.

formica top

storage

The Importance of Accuracy When Stretching Cloths

The importance of stretching all soft cloths accurately, with all four corners at right angles, cannot be over-emphasized, as indeed all scenery needs to be accurate. However, once a cloth has been stretched, primed and dried, it will have taken on that shape forever, and as it will be hung on a perfectly horizontal bar on stage, there quite simply cannot afford to be mistakes.

An advantage of frame-painting is that a better idea of the final effect can be appreciated, as it is hung up in place already, as opposed to being on a floor, where lighting differences are created whilst the work is being observed in this position.

Putting Up a Cloth

Most made-up cloths will have a pocket along the bottom, hemmed sides, and web and ties along the top, which are used to tie the cloth to the hanging bars.

The first process in hanging a cloth to a given frame, whether it is a proper working frame or one that has been built especially for a temporary measure, is to check that it is square or, in other words, that each corner is 90 degrees and that the battens that make up the frame are straight. Never assume that they will be, as time, wood and paint mixed together are a natural recipe for warping. To do this you will have to measure the width of the overall top batten first, then find the centre of this and mark it. Placing your plumb-line on this point and dropping it to the bottom will create a perfectly correct vertical. Both outside verticals can now be checked by the use of measurements taken from the marked centre at the top and bottom of the cloth. To check that any horizontal is

107

correct, a spirit-level is used. An alternative method is to take a measurement from corner to corner of the diagonals of the given frame, which should both be the same if the frame is perfectly square. A frame will most probably not be the correct size for the cloth that you want to hang, so a number of wooden battens will have to be added. In professional studios, a number of lengths of battens are always kept for this precise reason. Ideally you will want to make a made-to-measure frame, based on the given size of your cloth, but make sure that each piece of wood is extremely well fixed to the main frame, preferably by using 4–6in nails to ensure this. Once the frame is ready, the cloth can be put up. First, make sure that the floor around the frame is clean, and preferably keep a piece of clean polythene to place along the whole length of the frame for both putting up and getting the cloth down. (When working from a bridge, the cloth will have to lie on this, and the same goes for the gantry.) A made-up cloth will arrive from the suppliers folded up into a small bundle in the traditional method.

This method allows the cloth to be more easily transported, as well as opened directly onto the stage to tie on to the hanging bars. Open the bundle and look for the correct side and edge to be affixed first, starting from either the top-left or right-hand side of the cloth. This is then nailed or stapled along the length of the top

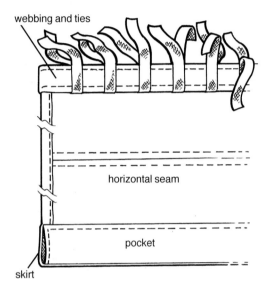

webbing and ties

horizontal seam

pocket

skirt

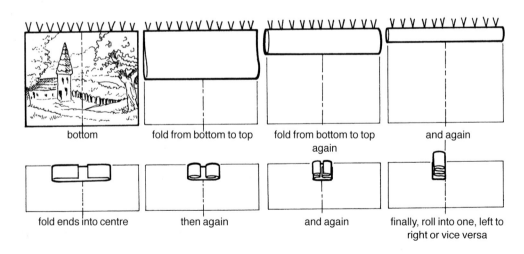

bottom

fold from bottom to top

fold from bottom to top again

and again

fold ends into centre

then again

and again

finally, roll into one, left to right or vice versa

(Above left) A made-up cloth.
(Above) How to fold up a cloth.

How to Take a Cloth off the Frame

It is worth describing at this point, how to take a cloth off the frame once the painting is done. First, remove all staples or nails around the two sides and bottom. Remove some of the top, but leave enough to hold the weight of the cloth when hanging freely. With the frame up, pull out the bottom edge about a metre (or yard), so that it lays on the floor or gantry. Using two people, or more if it is a very wide cloth, hold the edges at either end of the cloth, and allow the frame to move down slowly, whilst pulling the cloth into a concertina. Only when there is a neat and regular pile on the floor, with barely a hint of a crease, can the remaining nails be removed. Do not be afraid to start again, as it is important that it is done well. Finally, fold the length of cloth into a smaller bundle using the very same method as given for the floor.

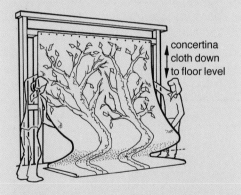

concertina
cloth down
to floor level

How to take a cloth off a paint frame, bridge or gantry.

of the cloth. (This measurement should be given on all artwork, technical drawings and the cloths themselves.) Ideally two people are needed for this, though one can do it! You will have to learn to judge whether or not a cloth is the right size for minor inconsistencies, as it can be difficult to measure such a large piece of loose fabric, and do not make the mistake of presuming that it will be made up to the exact requirements. A certain amount of juggling can be used where a cloth has minor differences, such as adjusting the frame slightly, but for larger errors, talk to the production manager or the suppliers. Remember that canvasses will always shrink a great deal, unlike gauzes, wools and velours, and that the webbing sewn into the top of a cloth and any hemming will always tighten the fabric and make it more difficult to stretch. Once the top of the cloth is securely fixed, the frame can be raised, or the gantry lowered, in order to let the cloth hang out completely. The next step is to put a staple or nail in each bottom corner before nailing out the rest of the cloth. This should be done starting with the top, then the bottom and finally the sides, placing the nails or staples about a hands width apart, and always well in from the edge of the cloth, so as to reduce the risk of tearing as the material shrinks during the priming process. A good tip is to place the first nails in the middle of each side, and subsequently work from middle to middle to ensure an even tension throughout. Try and remember to remove the cords before the next step, which is to prime!

The Floor Method

The most favourable aspect of floor-painting is that it allows for watery painting, where lots of splashing and washes of paint can be used to obtain certain effects. Another effective method is to utilize the texture already on the floor into the painting, in the same way that a brass rubbing is done, although there may well be certain paint effects that certainly do not

batten, using only a few nails or staples at this point, and pulling the cloth to the measured width required. Use a length of string or nylon cord as a more accurate line to which the cloth is pulled, on both the sides as well as the bottom

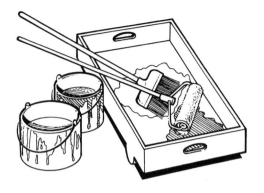

A paint tray.

removal. Another method of obtaining accurate lines is to ping a chalk line, but you must take care that this line can be clearly seen and also that it will not be rubbed out in the process of putting the cloth down. It is really important that all made-up cloths are stretched out extremely accurately, as the successful hanging of them on stage is completely dependent on this initial stretching out and priming. The cloth can now be nailed out, using the same order as a cloth on a frame. First, the top, then the bottom, and finally the sides, using the same middle-to-middle method to ensure an even tension. For cloths that have no hems or sewn edges, an efficient way of reducing the risk of tearing due to shrinkage is to lay down thin wooden battens on top of the cloth, all along the edge and nailing down through this.

require this! Disadvantages include the constant effort required to keep the surface clean, and the sheer physicality needed while working at this angle for a long time. Care must be taken when placing any buckets of paint on the actual cloth and it is highly recommended that a paint tray be used to house all of these as a way of minimizing the risk of spillage.

As far as possible, try to keep most buckets off a cloth altogether, although it is impossible at times. The other potential problem is that during the priming process, or any painting where there is no prime, the cloth can stick to the floor. In the description on priming, a technique for overcoming this is given.

Stretching a Cloth on the Floor

In Chapter 12, a description is given on a practical guide for using the Pythagorean theory, otherwise known as the 3:4:5 method. Having created a near-perfect right-angle on the floor using this method, lines can now be created to which the cloth can be nailed. Once the right-angle is established, this can be marked out with a long piece of string or nylon cord extending from one measurement to another, by hammering in a nail halfway to hold the strings. If staples are preferred, hold the stapler at an angle to achieve the same effect; this allows for subsequent easy

A Word About Methods

Finally, a word about methods. For both of these descriptions a particular method has been described. Like most crafts and techniques there can be more than one method, and each person may eventually discover their own preferred one. The inexperienced must not be confused by the fact that there may well be many different ways of doing things, at the same time as being told being told that there is only one way of doing any set task! A lot can be learned from the various methods that different scenic artists or studios use, which can only be beneficial to both the inexperienced as well as to the experienced scenic artist, as any improvement on any skill is an advantage.

PREPARATION AND PRIMING OF MATERIALS

The correct preparation of all materials that require this process is vital. The importance of this cannot be stressed too highly, as an incorrect process can lead to potential disaster due to the fact that any subsequent painting may be entirely ruined, either by quite literally falling off or becoming completely tainted. A list is given here of the individual preparations and primers needed for the scenic materials mentioned in this chapter, as well as the textural surfaces described in the chapter on textures.

Priming

This description refers to the use of prime for soft cloths, and fabric-covered flattage.

There is an important distinction to be made when describing exactly what prime or sizing does. It is not intended as a coating, but as a method of penetrating all the pores of a fabric in order to prepare them for subsequent continuous layers of paints. The way in which this is achieved is by permanently shrinking the fibres in order to create a smooth and workable surface for all subsequent painting processes. Without a good prime, an even coverage of paint would not be possible. The ways of priming these materials is either by the traditional method of a glue-size mix or, as is more commonly used now, the widely available emulsion paints and acrylic primers. The advantage of the traditional method of glue-sizing is that any subsequent wetting of the fabric will continue to re-tighten the fibres, which is particularly beneficial for canvassed flattage. The disadvantages are that this method is more time-consuming and a heat source is needed in order to prepare the size. Any prime for theatrical use needs to be as flexible as possible, and the emulsion and acrylic alternatives are designed to be especially so. Specific primers are not particularly cheap, and a cheaper alternative is to use scenic emulsion paint and then apply the mixture in a thorough and methodical fashion, so as to ensure a good coverage.

Applying Prime

Make sure that the mix is the right consistency. The only way to truly test any mix is to do a test sample: dry it with a heat gun and see how the

Tips for Priming

A prime can also be sprayed on, but a good tip is to get a fellow painter to follow on with a large dry brush and quite literally work the prime into the fabric. Observe that the nap of the fabric is reduced. An important point to remember is that when a cloth or piece of scenery has started to be primed, it must be finished in that session, rather than left until later, so leave plenty of time for larger areas.

Another handy tip is that when priming a cloth on the floor, once the actually painting or spraying is finished, lift a corner and blow in air from an air gun or even a hairdryer to lift the fabric from the floor. This will prevent it from sticking to the floor.

mix has covered the canvas. On a scenic canvas there should be a complete absence of what are known as 'holidays' or tiny holes. You will soon become accustomed to the feel of any prime on your brush, and know when it seems to readily glide or take to the surface or not! Drying off a sample will also give an indication of whether the mix is too thick and will crack, or whether it is too thin and will show up lots of holidays. Doing a test sample will also help you to check the flexibility, as well as colour, if need be.

Preparation of Size

To prepare size, first soak the glue in water, preferably overnight: use approximately 1 part glue to 5 parts water, until it has become a jelly and soaked up all the water. A double boiler filled with water is now required, and this is placed onto a direct heat. The lumps of jelly are melted, and further water added to dilute. The success of the mix depends on passing the thumb and finger test: wet fingers and thumb with the mixture and keep patting together until they feel really *tacky*. If the mix is too strong it will glue your fingers together, and if it is too weak, you will not be aware of any tackiness. The addition of 'whiting', a refined calcium, to glue-size, makes traditional gesso and is also an excellent primer for scenic canvas. The consistency of this should then run from a stick in a continuous stream without dripping.

To Prime or Not to Prime

Canvasses: all canvasses require priming, unless specifically requested not too for an alternative effect.

Floor cloth: traditionally these are painted with dyes in order that they remain as flexible as possible. If following this method, it is wise to firstly wash the surface over with brushes with a very weak solution of water and a tiny bit of washing-up liquid – this breaks up the water-resisting coating that is there to make this particular fabric waterproof (these fabrics are used for sails in yachts). If a prime is required, make sure that all seams are really penetrated, as the shrinkage on this fabric is terrific, as well as making sure that the mix is as thin as can be allowed in order to keep the flexibility of the cloth.

Calicos and sheeting: these can either be primed or not, depending on the particular requirements of the designer or scenic artist. If

A large brush is used to apply prime.

a prime is to be used, both materials need to be stretched more tightly than the canvasses, as there is not as much shrinkage.

Those fabrics that do not require prime include: filled cloth, silks, velvets/velours, wool serges and hessians.

PVC: the only possible preparation needed on these materials is that they are kept as clean and grease-free as possible. The most important point to mention here is that an additive must be added to your paint mix in order that:

* the paint adheres well to the surface; and
* the cloth does not stick to itself when subsequently folded or rolled.

The way to achieve this is to add a small mixture, such as Covent Garden Primer (available from specialist scenic suppliers), which can also be used for other clear plastics, rubber flooring and vac forms. The most important point to mention here is that there is no fixed formula for success, other than testing on the actual surface to be applied until you feel confident that the paint will adhere correctly. Too little and it will obviously scrape off with a fingernail; too much and the material will stick to itself.

Polyvinyl metallics: if any kind of painting is needed here, the method given for PVC is recommended. Make sure that all surfaces are as dust-free as possible before commencing work. Invasive glues are not recommended for sticking.

Contra: this textural material is usually stuck onto another surface such as canvas. A resin-based glue is recommended for sticking, if required.

Metals: all metals must be cleaned first with a metal degreaser. Primers and coatings are available from a number of different brands, such as Etch Primers, Two Pot Etch Primers and Red

Oxides, all of which serve a variety of different metals. These are extremely toxic and require the use of organic vapour masks, and all work should be undertaken in well-ventilated surroundings. Alternatively, there are now a number of water-based acrylic enamels that do not require such drastic health and safety measures and are arguably preferable. These are available from most specialist scenic suppliers and good commercial paint suppliers.

Wood and wood-based products: due to the highly absorbent nature of wood, it is necessary to treat all surfaces with a sealer to block out any natural stains and resins. Shellac, button polish or white knotting is ideal. However, there are now a number of water-based acrylic enamels available as alternatives, though they are not as reliable.

Plaster and textural surfaces: if you are intending to put texture on any wooden surface, you must make sure that this has been properly sealed; if this is not done properly the texture is liable to fall off. Then, depending on the type of effect required, you may or may not prime. No prime will mean that the surfaces are far more absorbent, but when a prime is required, any acrylic scenic primer will do, or a thinned-out scenic emulsion glaze or PVA.

Vac forms and pre-cast moulds: prior to any painting, a coating is normally required and the method given for PVC is recommended. Make sure that all surfaces are as dust-free as possible before commencing work.

Polystyrene: due to the potential fire risk of these materials, they must at all times be protected with an appropriate fire-retardant coating. A description of muslin scrimming is given in Chapter 15, which is highly recommended for any scenery that is also likely to undergo a lot of wear and tear. An effective alternative method is to use one of the new flame-retardant protective coatings now available.

Foams/sponges: the description for polystyrene applies to these materials, except for muslin scrimming.

Vinyl floorings: if any kind of painting is needed here, the method given for PVC is recommended. Make sure that all surfaces are as dust-free as possible before commencing work.

Perspex/polycarbonate: a material often used for scenic purposes. Make sure that the surface is as dust-free as possible before painting. Most scenic paints will not adhere directly to this surface, so an appropriate binder added to standard scenic colours or specialist paint for plastic surfaces is recommended. FEVs can also be used on this surface.

Fibreglass: a task often given to scenic artists is that of painting props. You will therefore need to know how to prep the surfaces prior to any painting. A good sanding is normally required, taking care to use the appropriate PPE. Any filling that is required is best done with a two-part resin-based filler, and the entire surface then wiped free of dust before any subsequent processes are started. An appropriate coating would be Covent Garden Primer or any other brand that is designed to have superior fixing qualities. Check with any of the specialist scenic manufacturers listed at the end of the book for details.

Jesmonite: this is a relatively new and revolutionary material now available on the market, which is a water-based fibreglass system, and so contains no harmful solvents. The appropriate PPE should be worn when handling, and a water-based clear acrylic coating is used as a sealer. Subsequent painting can then be done using standard scenic paints.

12 DRAWING

This chapter provides an explanation of the drawing skills required for the scenic artist. It begins with a consideration of the equipment needed and how to grid up a model, understand scale and mark out the scenery. Explanations and tips are given on various different drawing processes involved, including skills in drawing architecture, understanding basic perspective, figurative drawing and basic lettering. The use of specialized scenic devices, such as pounces, stencils and mousetraps, is also explained, as well as the use of overhead projectors.

Imagine the foundations of a building, and how strong and precise they need to be in order for building to be erected above them. Without their accuracy the building would become weak and most probably fall down. This analogy can be used to describe the vital importance of good drawing in relation to scenic art. This is certainly true of a great many creative skills, but the sheer scale of the painted images means that any inaccuracies are quite literally magnified! In this chapter the various tools used by the scenic artist are explained, and the various drawing processes involved in re-creating the designs.

TOOLS

A list is given here of the main drawing tools that a scenic artist uses. A few of these can be quite expensive to buy but, if the budget can stretch this far, it will be a wise investment: so long as they are well looked after they should last a lifetime. A more economical way of collecting them is either by searching in a second-hand market stall or even making certain tools, as will be explained.

* **Scale ruler**: 1:20, 25, 33⅓, 50, 75 and 100. A foot ruler can be used for the 1:24 scale.
* **Tape-measure**: ideally 30m (100ft) long, and preferably made of fibreglass coated with PVC. Metric and imperial as standard. This should certainly last a lifetime.
* **Metre ruler**: metric and imperial as standard again.
* **Straight edges:** on a stick, if working on the floor, with bevelled edges. These can be bought but are easily made.
* **Trammel heads**: used for drawing large arcs and circles on the floor. An economical alternative is a long piece of straight wood and a nail, with charcoal or pen attached to the other end.
* **Roofing square**: the size of this is particularly useful for scenic work.
* **Spirit-level**: a godsend for marking out horizontals on a frame!
* **Stanley knife**: for regular sharpening of your charcoal/chalk; a spare blade is also useful.
* **Chalk lines**: for making accurate straight lines, otherwise known as *ping* lines. A cheaper alternative is a long piece of parcel-quality string, stored on a piece of wooden offcut.
* **Boxes of charcoal**: these come in various sizes, and all can be used.

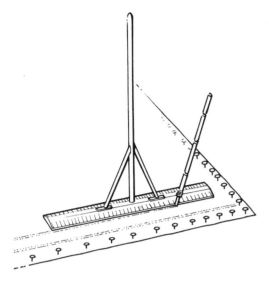

A straight edge.

* **Pencils**.
* **Large compass**: a cheap alternative is simply to use a taut piece of string attached at one end that acts as the pivot. Use a safety pin for cloths on a frame, and a nail for the floor.
* **Chalk stick for drawing on the floor**: these can be bought, but most scenic artists

use the age-old method of a bamboo stick, spliced at one end to hold the charcoal, using an elastic band, and made to measure!

* **Flogger**: this describes the tool used for simply beating away the lines you no longer require. Made up from a wooden handle with strips of cloth attached to the other end.
* **Set of drawing tools**: to include set-square, compass and protractor.
* **Calculator**: if you are a master at arithmetic then you probably will not need this, but there will be those who will find it invaluable.
* **Selection of writing implements**: pencils, drawing pens, chinagraph pencils and marker pens.
* **Pounce wheel**.

This list gives the reader a selection of tools that a well-equipped scenic studio should have. There are obviously going to be times when a scenic artist may be working away from the studio, or in a venue where it would be inconvenient to transport every piece of equipment. In such cases, it is a good idea to do much of the complex drawing beforehand in a studio with

A flogger and chalk stick.

access to all tools. The work can then be transported in the form of cartoons, tracings or perhaps stencils, or in whatever form is required for a particular job. Your personal toolbox should have a selection of basic drawing tools that will be quite adequate for the jobs done on site. These drawing devices will be explained later in this chapter.

DRAWING PROCESSES

At the first model-showing, a scenic artist will have looked analytically at the design to work out the processes to be involved. At this point, apart from observing the painted effects, materials and textures, it is also important to be aware of any drawing processes that may be required. Think ahead of just how certain effects may be created, such as a repeat of a wallpaper design or painted brickwork, although there may be certain designs that will involve little or no drawing at all.

The sheer scale and amount of work involved in scenic art means that it is often necessary to use time-saving and economical devices. These specialist drawing techniques and devices are therefore another type of tool,

whose purpose is to ease any difficulties that may arise, or quite simply make the job easier.

The drawing processes required in scenic art are for constructed pieces of scenery, such as flattage and floors, or for the soft cloths and props that may need painting (artists will often be required to paint props, especially in amateur theatre). In the commercial scenic workshops and in-house theatre studios, scenic art and props are different departments, and props are often painted by the prop maker themselves. However, this is not always the case and the scenic artist will often be called upon for this job.

The first thing to do is to gather all relevant information together. This will include the relevant model pieces, technical drawings and any references that the designer may have provided. Make sure that the model pieces are protected with acetate, as this can also be used as part of the drawing process.

Technical Drawings
Technical drawings are what a designer will have produced as part of their design. These are the detailed and precise drawings to scale, of all the components that go to make up the

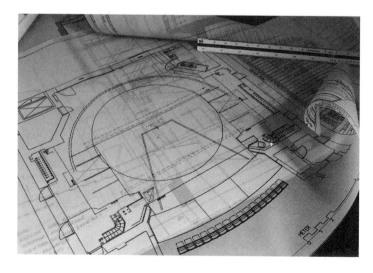

Technical drawings.

When working in metric it is important to get used to thinking in millimetres, especially as the scenic carpenters work in this form. Try not to use, or think in, centimetres as it can be confusing for all! When in imperial, simply use feet and inches.

whole set. This includes measurements and relevant design requirements, such as a choice of a particular moulding for the carpenters or a detail of ornament for the scenic artist. A note of warning: it is really important to bear in mind that, regardless of how experienced a designer is, mistakes can occur in the technical drawings. It must become second nature to double-check all the measurements. A seemingly small mistake in a wrong measurement can be disastrous! In most amateur theatre productions there will probably be no technical drawings, but sooner or later the reader will come across them and it is really important to understand what they are and, more importantly, how to read them.

SCENIC DRAWING METHODS

There are three ways of drawing out on scenery that includes soft as well as hard pieces. These are:

* **A gridding system**: the artwork and actual piece of scenery is divided into a series of co-ordinating scaled-up squares. The scenic artist then uses this method as a way of transposing the image to the scenery by referring to the gridded artwork (*see* diagram, page 119). This is ideal for a lot of artwork, such as landscapes, but can cause some confusion for any design requiring a great number of lines, such as architecture.
* **A plotting system**: using a scale ruler, a scenic artist works out a series of points from a number of carefully worked out vertical and horizontal lines, which are used to build up the rest of a drawing. This is useful for both architecture and large curves (*see* diagrams below and overleaf).
* **The use of freehand drawing**: certain designs often come without precise details of ornamentation or may require figurative work that is best done freehand once its correct position has been established, or quite simply by designing your own stencils.

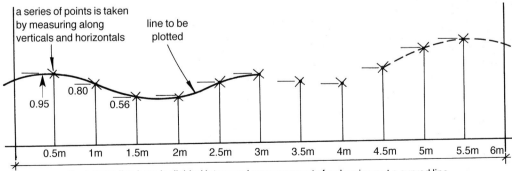

the bottom line here is divided into equal measurements for drawing out a curved line

This shows the scenic system of drawing out a curved line by plotting.

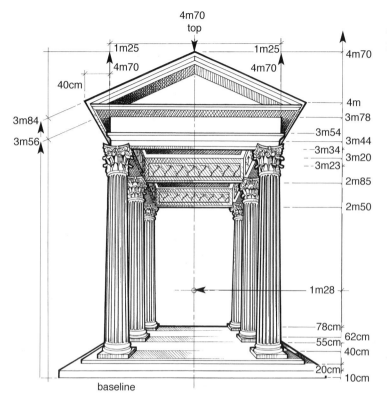

4m70
top

1m25

1m25

4m70

4m70

40cm

4m70

3m84

3m56

4m

3m78

3m54

3m44

3m34

3m20

3m23

2m85

2m50

1m28

78cm

62cm

55cm

40cm

20cm

10cm

baseline

This shows a typical architectural plotting method.

GRIDDING UP A DESIGN AND A SCENIC CLOTH ON A PAINT FRAME

Gridding Up the Design

It is easier to grid up a three-dimensional model by using the technical drawings as reference, and using the model for colour and painting references. The first thing to do, after covering the original design in acetate, is to ascertain what scale the design is in. (Some designs may only be copies of the original, and it is not necessary to be so protective of these.) This is normally clearly stated on the technical drawings. The most commonly used (approximately 90 per cent of theatre designers) is 1:25. A prop will normally be drawn in 1:10.

For those readers who have never worked to scale before, it is really quite simple. On the scale ruler, a 1m unit represents 25m on the actual width or height of cloth or scenery (the

Drawing for Other Departments

It is important to mention that a scenic artist may often be required to do a certain amount of drawing out for both scenic carpenters as well as metalworkers. For example, a tree that is being constructed out of metal or a curved piece of wooden set, will require the structure of it drawn out either directly onto the workshop floor or as a template beforehand.

How to grid-up the design.

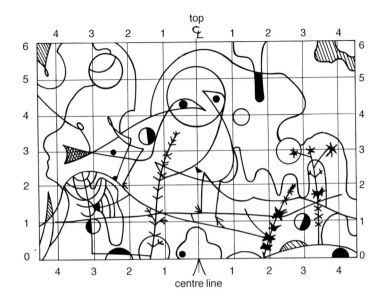

same principle applies to imperial or metric). Taking 1:25 as the scale, draw an accurate line around the image. The next process is to find the exact centre line along the top and bottom horizontal, either by measuring or by using a piece of paper folded to the same length of the image and folded exactly in half. This is how the Egyptians built the pyramids, so it is a long and trusted technique! Working from each side of the centre line mark out 1m divisions to the edge of the design with neat precise marks, from the scale ruler. This is where a sharpened chinagraph pencil comes in handy, or an indelible thin pen, as the model will undergo a lot of handling. From the bottom to the top of the design, mark out the same divisions. Repeat this process along the top line, always working outwards from the centre line. Although 1m divisions are the normal measurements for scenic work, this can vary depending on the complexity of a design.

Draw the grid from these lines, and then number the boxes as shown, which will give each square its identity. This is important for when drawing out, as it is easy to either start drawing in the wrong box or get lost in the process! There may often be more than one scenic artist drawing out on a cloth and so this will help to avoid disorientation.

Gridding Up the Cloth

The cloth, which will have been stretched out either on the floor or a frame, must be gridded up following the same processes as used for scaling up your design. The lines of the grid can either be made using 'ping' chalk lines, a long piece of cord or strong cotton. Some scenic artists prefer to use this method, but it is purely a matter of personal preference.

There are two main reasons why a scenic artist always works from the bottom edge of a design and the actual piece of scenery, as well as from the centre line. First, because of any discrepancies there may be in the cloth or design measurements. A designer will have worked out the sight lines and knows how much of an image is to be seen, and by working from the centre you can rely on being accurate. Second, because the bottom edge of

119

a cloth or any piece of scenery will always be positioned on the stage floor, which is a guaranteed horizontal. A word of warning: always check the measurements of a made-up cloth or scenery, with those from the technical drawings and the model piece itself, as there are often discrepancies. It is now time to start drawing out.

Tips on Drawing Out

Here are a few tips on drawing out on soft cloths and scenery, whether using the frame or floor method.

* If working alone, attach a large safety pin to one end of the chalk line to aid in pinging the grid lines.
* It is very important that when marking out a number of given measurements over a long distance, for example twenty 1m squares or fifty 10cm marks, it is better to use a long tape-measure rather than use a metre rule. This is because the measurements are far more liable to become inaccurate over a long distance, as one mistake created at the beginning will become greatly multiplied over a greater area.
* Another method for marking out a lot of regular measurements, such as bricks or floor tiles, is to mark your measurements all out on to a long piece of wood first, which will save a lot of time and will ensure accuracy.
* When working on the floor, keep a piece of old canvas or other fabric at the edge to wipe feet on, as it is important that the drawing is kept as clean as possible.
* If working on a design that requires a lengthy curve to be drawn using the floor method, a length of heavy rope, compressor hose or other such item can be laid out along the plotting points, which will help in creating a flowing and consistent line.
* When drawing out on any sections of scenery on the floor that are designed to be

linked together, make sure they all line up exactly along the bottom line by using a piece of string, and actually nailing them in this exact position. This is really important for starting any drawing, and for subsequent painting.
* When working on any scenery that is larger than the paintshop floor, use a process of rotation. Ensure that every piece is marked individually on the back, as well as with arrows showing up- or downstage, and that there is always one finished drawing piece laid down with the new additions to be to kept as a continuing point of reference.

BASIC ARCHITECTURAL DRAWING AND PERSPECTIVE

Having a good basic understanding of architecture, geometry and perspective is extremely important for a scenic artist, and a brief description here will hopefully inspire the reader to study further. Being able to recognize and understand the basic principles of the classical orders of architecture from Greek, through to Roman and Renaissance, along with early civilizations such as the Egyptians, will offer a skill in understanding architectural rudiments such as proportion, rhythm and scale.

It is really important to appreciate that it is only by understanding how an object works, whether organic or inorganic, that a scenic artist will ever be able to re-interpret it into a two- or three-dimensional form. Further study in any of these fields cannot help but improve an artist's work, by way of sketching, reading or even taking a short course in a field of particular interest. A number of diagrams with explanations are presented that illustrate the main shapes and methods. Anyone wishing to study it further will find it a rewarding subject.

The classical order of architecture: (left) Doric, from the Parthenon; (centre) Ionic, from the Erechtheion; (right) Corinthian, from the Monument of Lysicrates.

121

GEOMETRY

Pythagorean Theory

Pythagorean theory, or better known among scenic artists as the 3:4:5 method, is probably the most useful piece of geometry that a scenic artist will ever learn. Due to the need for consistently accurate squaring-up of all cloths and scenery, it is imperative that this is learnt and remembered. The theory states the square of the length of the hypotenuse on a right-angled triangle is equal to the sum of the squares of the lengths of the other two sides. This is illustrated in the diagram below.

The example shown here is using particular measurements. To make a right-angled triangle, using a measured ratio of 3:4:5m (any unit of measurement, such as feet, can be applied):

* establish a line A to B, of a measurement of 3m;
* using A as a centre, create a 4m arc;
* using B as centre, create an arc of 5m;
* the intersection of these two arcs is point C;
* join A and C, to obtain a right angle.

It is worth mentioning that for greater accuracy whilst using this method, as large measurements as possible should be used.

This theory can be applied in a number of ways:

* as an accurate way of squaring-up a large area, which is particularly useful when working in a space that has no recognizable straight lines or right angles, such as a rented floor space, not originally intended for scenic purposes;
* as a way of checking if a cloth hung on a frame is square;
* as a means of checking if a given object itself, such as a piece of flat scenery or a paint frame, is square;
* as a means of finding an accurate centre line on a cloth, for example where there may not be a perfectly square frame, as is often the case.

How to Draw an Ellipse
This is useful when drawing ornamentation, carpets, picture frames:

* establish the dimensions of the ellipse whose major diameter is AB, and minor diameter is CD;
* the mid-point perpendicular bisector of these two is E;

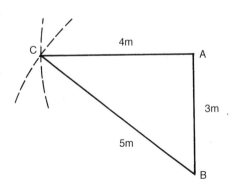

Pythagorean theory, otherwise known as the 3:4:5 method.

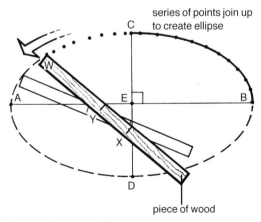

How to draw an ellipse.

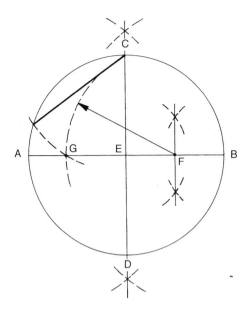

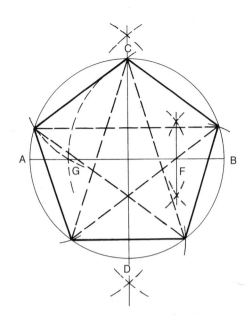

* using a straight edge, such as a piece of wood, mark one end point W, placing it along the line of AB and mark off point E onto your straight edge, creating point X;
* place your straight edge with point W at point C, along the line CD, and mark off point E, to create point Y;
* points X and Y are used as anchor points to plot along lines AB and CD, to create the arc of an ellipse, at point W;
* finally, connect the points together to create an ellipse.

How to Construct a Star within a Pentagon
This one is for all those night-time starry cloths:

* draw a circle of any given measurement;
* draw in the diameter AB;
* draw in the perpendicular diameter CD, to create mid-point E;
* bisect at EB to get mid-point F;
* using FC as the radius, draw in an arc CG;
* with C as the centre, and CG as the radius, draw an arc through the circle to point H;
* draw in a straight line between H and C, which becomes one equal side of the pentagon;

How to draw a pentagon.

* find the remaining four sides by marking off width HC around the circle.

How to Construct a Hexagon
This is useful for drawing out tiled floors:

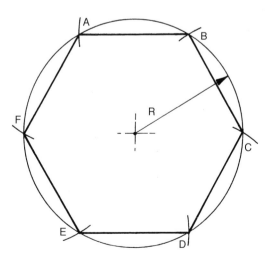

How to draw a hexagon.

123

* to construct a hexagon of side length R, draw a circle of radius R;
* swing arcs along the circumference also using radius R, to form the points of the hexagon;
* finally, join up the points to complete the hexagon.

Basic Linear Perspective

Unlike an architect, whose job it is to render a perspective drawing from scratch, the scenic artist's job is to analyse an existing design, recognize its elements and basically be able to reproduce it accurately many times larger. Without understanding how linear perspective works, a scenic artist could not expect to paint any designs that use it. The first laws of perspective are thought to have originated in early Greek plays but were more realized in the Renaissance period when an understanding of space and distance became formalized in geometrical studies, as seen by the work of theatre designer Sebastiano Serlio. This section is intended to simply introduce the reader to the fundamentals of linear perspective; further study is highly recommended.

What Exactly is Linear Perspective?

Linear perspective is a geometrical system by which a three-dimensional space, and the people and objects within it, are represented on a two-dimensional surface.

There are several main points that govern the way in which a perspective drawing is constructed, and these are:

* the station point (SP): this is the position of the eye of the spectator (*see* the diagram above);
* cone of vision (COV): this is what the human eye can see within its field of vision;
* picture plane (PP): this is seen as the 'backdrop' on which all the perspective lines converge towards the vanishing point;

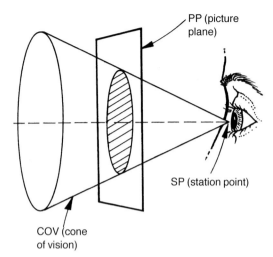

The cone of vision.

* vanishing point (VP): this is where the projecting lines from the objects within the picture converge to an infinite point, always at a distance from the spectator;
* the horizon line (HL): in any field of vision there is always an horizon line, which is the line between sky and land. It is often obscured in everyday vision by buildings and trees, but think of an ocean or an long open road – it is always at eye height and horizontal.

One-Point Perspective

This is the simplest form of drawing perspective, where there is one vanishing point on the horizon line. In order to draw out correctly any perspective from a given design, the scenic artist must first of all ascertain where the vanishing point is. This is done by creating converging lines to the horizon line as illustrated right.

Two-Point/Multi-Perspective

This is a more complex arrangement where the objects are seen obliquely and two or more

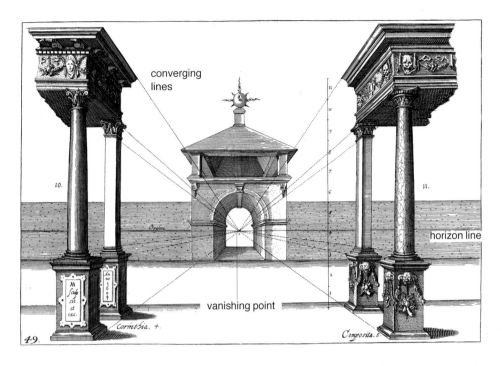

(Above) An illustration to show one-point perspective.
(Below) An illustration to show two-point and multi-perspective.

faces of the same object are seen. As a result, there are two or more vanishing points, which are both on the horizontal picture line. There can also be vertical vanishing points, where tall buildings appear to taper into the sky. A cathedral illustrates this well, with lofty high-vaulted ceilings, a nave, side windows and aisles.

DRAWING THE FIGURE

Being able to draw the human figure is an important aspect of a scenic artist's drawing abilities. There may well be a number of occasions when this skill is required, and to both paint and draw the figure can be an enormously pleasurable experience. First and foremost is understanding human anatomy, and once this is mastered, the student will grasp how the

Working on figurative work.

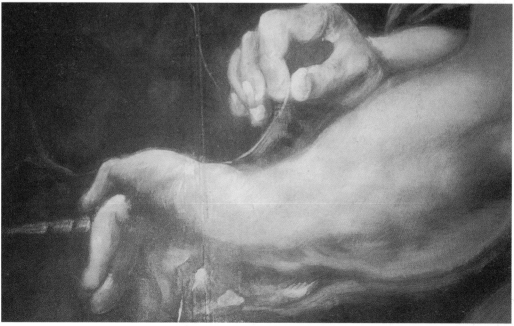

(Above) A good way of improving your figurative drawing is to attend life classes.
(Below) Detail.

whole figure itself works. It is not possible to draw the figure when there is little understanding of what goes on under the surface.

If you have already done a lot of figurative drawing, it will be good practise to start drawing in a much larger scale, so as to meet the scenic requirements. Also, practice drawing with a chalk stick, both for floor and frame painting (though some scenics prefer not to use this method). From a personal point of view, being able to stand back from any drawing is important, and once having mastered drawing with a chalk stick it will make the whole process much easier. For those who have less experience in figurative work, it is never too late to take up regular life-drawing classes or, more economically, get friends or family to pose! Sketching is also a good way of practising and, if regularly kept up, a tremendous improvement will soon be noticed.

Basic Lettering

The tools that are needed for this are as follows:

* scale ruler
* tape-measure
* set-square
* straight edge
* chalk lines.

To be able to draw and subsequently paint any form of lettering in scenic art, it is necessary to understand a core system of basic facts, which once grasped, all future work should be relatively simple – no matter how complex the lettering.

Primarily it is important to know that a scenic artist will often have the job of deciding what font the letters are going to be drawn in. A designer will not necessarily have provided this information, so keeping a book of fonts is highly recommended as part of your reference library.

Listed here, with a brief explanation to each section, are the basics:

* A 'font' describes the particular style of lettering: such as 'Times New Roman', or 'Arial Black'. There are literally hundreds to choose from.
* Upper case and lower case refer to capital letters, and non-capital letters. The terms 'upper' and 'lower' refer to the position of the type cases when printing compositors' set by hand: the capitals, being needed less frequently, were positioned further away at the top of a sloping desk.
* With reference to size, a capital letter is referred to as the H height, whilst the lower case is referred to as the X height.
* Any letter above the X-height line is known as an ascender.
* Any letter that moves into position below the X height is known as a descender.

An example of the kind of lettering a scenic artist may be required to do.

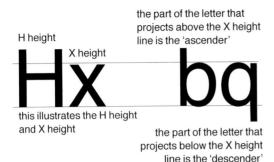

H height
X height

this illustrates the H height and X height

the part of the letter that projects above the X height line is the 'ascender'

the part of the letter that projects below the X height line is the 'descender'

A B C D E F G H I J K L
O M O P Q R S T U V W
X Y Z
a b c d e f g h i j k l m n
o p q r s t u v w x y z
£&?!
1 2 3 4 5 6 7 8 9 0

upper case
lower case

Cc

upper and lower case refer to CAPITAL and non-capital letters

sans serif
serif

SS

A B C D E F G H I J K L
O M O P Q R S T U V W
X Y Z
£&?! 1 2 3 4 5 6 7 8 9 0

Basic lettering for the scenic artist.

Two examples of fonts: above, Gill Sans; below, Photina.

✴ If one breaks down the simplest letter shapes in an alphabet, they become straight lines, circles and half-circles. The straight lines developed out of the first recognizable Roman 'carved' letters seen on the Trajan column AD 113, and the curves developed from the writings created by monks in scriptoriums using quill and brush.

The basic strokes of any letter form are the straight line, circle and half circle.

✴ Optical spacing: the spacing between letters is as important as each individual letter. In order to layout a word correctly, it would seem natural to divide the given width into equal measurements but, as most letters are of varying widths, this then looks incorrect. All professional sign writers rely on their trained eye to judge whether or not a word is correctly spaced, and in time you will too.

✴ Serif and sans serif: this refers to a letter that has a small line at the extremities of the main stroke in a type character, or not.

Given above are examples of two different fonts: Gill and Photina.

Gill is an extremely good example for a beginner to learn to draw and subsequently paint, as it easily reveals the rudimentary three shapes, as well as each letter being the same width.

129

Drawing Out Lettering

For a scenic artist drawing out any lettering, the processes are as follows:

* Having chosen a font, note the relationship between the height and width of the letters or work directly from a given scale. Having worked out a measurement for one letter, use this as an approximation for the rest.
* Draw out all horizontal lines. If working on a number of words, divide the widths approximately, according to the number of letters, allowing for ample margins if working on a sign.
* Sketch in the whole word or words, remembering that a scenic artist must learn to really observe what they are drawing, in the same way as they need to analyse the human form in life drawing. Therefore, think of this process as reproducing each and every characteristic of the given font.
* When confident that the spacing, character, widths of lines and so on, are pretty acceptable, then draw them in more accurately. It is a mistake to try and begin with a confidently finished letter at the very start.

Periodically stand back, as any mistakes are more easily seen from a distance.

Finally, a word about painting lettering. A sign-writer's brush is not a must in this respect, due to the variations in size. But it is important that the brush be well looked after, as frizzy edges are a major nuisance.

DRAWING DEVICES

Pouncing

For this, the following equipment is required:

* a pounce wheel;
* an old piece of polystyrene;
* brown paper;
* drawing materials, charcoal, pencils, etc.

This is the method of transferring any drawing on paper, otherwise known as a cartoon, to another surface, by means of dusting a coloured pigment through a number of tiny holes matching the image, that are created by the pounce wheel.

Ideally it is used for:

* Repetition of any design that needs to be duplicated.
* When working on a complex and time-consuming design that can be prepared earlier in the studios prior to using it onstage at the actual theatre perhaps, where there may be a lot less time given to execute the work.
* When working on a complex piece of drawing for a piece of scenery that requires to be kept extremely clean, as is often the case, this can become very messy when charcoal is used. It is therefore useful to prepare the drawing as a pounce and later transfer the image to the actual surface.

To make a pounce, first work out the size of the image required, allowing for a small overlap. Then using brown paper ideally, which is available in long rolls (900 × 250mm), make up the desired size, taping any edges together when required. Do not be put off by size, as it is quite easy to have a pounce up to 10m or

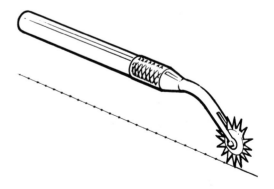

A pounce wheel.

more. Grid or plot out the drawing in the same way as was done on a cloth or piece of scenery. When finished, take a pounce wheel and literally pierce through the entire image until all lines have been covered. This should be done directly onto a piece of polystyrene, which can be moved around as the pounce wheel is used. Next, turn over the drawing and gently rub a piece of sandpaper over the back, so as to remove the excess bits of punctured paper. The pounce is now ready for using. The way in which the drawing is now transferred is by filling a small bag of muslin, at least a couple of layers thick, with any pigment. The pounce is now taped into its correct position and the muslin bag gently dabbed

(Right) This image needs to be repeated three times, therefore a pounce is ideal. Taken from Ornament *by Stuart Durant, published by Macdonald.*
(Below) A pounce being drawn out.

A pounce being used on the hung cloth.

over the image. A piece of charcoal drawn over the lines will also do, but experiment to find the most successful method. Once the pounce is removed, the entire drawing has been transferred onto the scenery, and all that remains to be done is to cleanly re-emphasize the lines, ready for painting.

Stencils

A stencil is a device by which an image can be transferred by painting or spraying through a series of shapes that have been cut out of a piece of waterproof card. This is yet another time-saving device, which is simple and highly efficient. It is used for the following reasons:

(Below) Stencils.

* any repetition of pattern, such as wallpaper designs, architectural mouldings or patterns, skyscraper windows, etc.;
* for use in lettering – this saves on messy drawing out, and the stencil is easily transferred to the given piece of scenery for painting or spraying;
* for use in conjunction with three-dimensional poly carving, as the image to be carved can be sprayed directly onto the surface, helping to create a clearer idea of the design.

The following equipment is required:

* stencil paper;
* surgical knives and blades;
* flat surface to work;
* drawing tools and a marker pen.

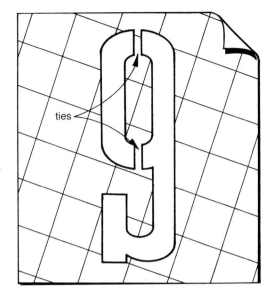

ties

Ideally, use ready made stencil paper, that has been pre-oiled and is, therefore, waterproof, in order to survive the subsequent wetting with paint. This is available from specialist art suppliers. This can be costly, so another method is to paint a piece of card with any shellac substance, front and back, in order to waterproof it. Important points to remember are:

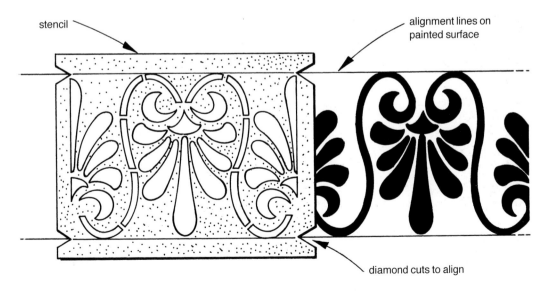

stencil

alignment lines on painted surface

diamond cuts to align

(Above) Cut out your stencil leaving ties to hold floating pieces intact.
(Below) Match up your lines with diamond cuts at each end of the stencil.

* where a pattern repeat is required, the design needs to be thought out as carefully as possible and designed so that it can be realigned time and again;
* any design for a stencil, however complex, needs to be simplified so that it can be cut out;
* once the image has been drawn out, it is a good idea to redraw it with a marker pen and create 'ties' to hold any floating pieces intact;
* the easiest way of then transferring this to the set piece is by a series of corresponding lines on both the stencil and the surface to be painted, which are then matched up by using small diamond-shaped cuts in the stencil.

Mousetraps

This is not a device for catching small, furry friends, but an alternative method for a quick and efficient way of tracing. They are useful because, having previously drawn the first of ten images on a cloth, for example, instead of repeating what was perhaps a lengthy process, a mousetrap can transfer the image more quickly and efficiently.

Ideally, they can be made up and kept in a paintshop. They are made from a simple wooden frame, with a piece of fine or scenic gauze stretched over tightly and stapled onto the edge. This is then held up to, or onto, the drawing on the cloth or piece of scenery, and traced over with a piece of charcoal. This can then be re-drawn as many times as required by moving the mouse trap to the desired area. When the gauze becomes too overdrawn and tatty, a new piece is simply stretched over the frame. They are ideal for simpler drawings.

Templates

A quick and ideal way of repeating a simple shape is to cut it out of a piece of thin wood or a stiff card and use this as a guide to make as many repeats as desired.

Overhead Projectors

It is important to mention the use of these despite the fact that many traditionalists will consider them to be an easy option method. The drawing that is done from these can never take the place of your own drawing skills, but in situations where time is short, they can be a bonus. As long as they are always treated in this

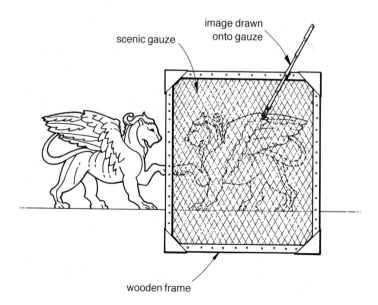

scenic gauze

image drawn onto gauze

wooden frame

Mousetraps.

way, and never seen as a replacement, then they fill a niche as a drawing 'device'. An example is shown in the photo of a set that needed a great number of names to be painted in a very short space of time. A projector was used for this very purpose by inking them in directly on to the set pieces, eliminating even the need for drawing!

Computer-Aided Printouts

A final word about drawing methods involves the use of computers as part of a scenic artist's reper- toire. In the same way that many designers use computers as part of their designs, a scenic artist may also embrace this use of technology in the twenty-first century. An entire design, or any image, can be scanned into the computer, adjust- ments made if needed, and the entire picture then printed out to scale. This can then be used for drawing out the scenery, in the same way as a pounce is used. It is, however, a costly process.

(Above) An overhead projector.
(Right) In this design for **Accrington Pals,** *by Neil Irish and directed by Graham Watts, over 300 names had to be painted in a tight time schedule. The use of an overhead projector proved invaluable here.*

13 Colour

This chapter looks at the many aspects of colour: its meanings, theories, terminology and history are discussed briefly, as well as a general explanation of how colour developed into the production of paints and dyes. Finally, scenic products are specifically considered, as well as the more widely available materials, and advice is given on buying, mixing and matching colours.

The poet Robert Browning wrote, 'Colours seen by candle light will not look the same by day', which sums up the theatrical use of colour, where an audience sees a stage set under an array of ever-changing and evocative lights, unlike the scenic artist who will have realized the design under quite different circumstances. In this chapter, colour will be discussed on practical, theoretical and historical levels. It is a fascinating and exciting subject that can only be touched on in a book like this, but will hopefully inspire the reader to delve far deeper as their work as a scenic artist progresses. It is highly recommended that further reading is done on the subject, and a reading list is given at the end of the book.

Colour is around us in every shape and form. Our surroundings, our moods and our lives in general are affected by the way in which colour is used, in both natural and manufactured ways. Take the colour red, for example, in its many guises: as the colour of blood, it symbolizes passion and fire, and is worn as a lipstick to enhance sensuality. Or the colour blue that conjures images of seas and skies, and is used in the painting of a Madonna's robes, depicting a rare and sacred colour. By these examples we can see that colour has been utilized to enhance an image or emotion further. It is a powerful tool. Here is a simple exercise to help emphasize this point. Below is a list of buildings, items and events that have been picked at random. Try and visualize each one:

* a can of Coca Cola;
* a mourner at a funeral;
* a New York cab;
* Barbie;
* a bride's wedding gown.

Apart from the actual object or event, an awareness of certain colours will also have left a memorable imprint on the reader's mind, in the order of:

Colour!

136

* red/white
* black/dark
* yellow
* pink
* white.

This demonstrates, in a small way, just how affected we are by colour and the way it can be to used – not only in a visual sense – but also as a emotional tool. It is in this form that the theatre designer will use colour. In order to convey emotions or images, colour plays an important role in their design, just as the shapes and meanings of the three-dimensional aspects of the set do as well. A scenic artist will, therefore, as artist and craftsmen in their own right, have a vital role to play in the understanding, sense and eventual re-creation of these colours.

A brief look at the history of colour shows us that as early as the Palaeolithic Period, around 2.5 to 3 million years ago, primitive humans used colour in an artistic sense. To think of these early pigments being used for creating images is a tremendously exciting thought. It seems obvious that art and the need to express oneself, have been around since the dawning of humankind. Since that time, when natural raw materials would have been ground down to use as a painting material, colour has undertaken the most amazing journey in humankind's quest for artistic expression. This brings us aptly to the point of explanation about what exactly colour is and, for creative purposes, in what form it can be found.

In order to have a good understanding, but above all, *feeling* for colour, it is common practice to teach the physics and theories of colour. This will be given here in a simple and straightforward manner. Like most practical subjects, there will often be a rather academic side to it but, in general, this analysing of the subject will help the student to understand the subject more fully. However, it needs to be stressed that an aspiring scenic artist can only really learn by experience and practice. In the immortal words of the great

scenic artist and designer Vladimir Polunin, painter to Diaghiliv, that to 'live and learn' is quite simply the best bit of advice a painter can be given (taken from his fascinating book *The Continental Method of Scene Painting*). Once started on the road to becoming a scenic artist, and the importance of observation and analysis is learned, the understanding of colour begins to occur quite naturally. It can be compared to the understanding of a foreign language: if this is studied only from textbooks, then it will be harder to truly conquer than if the language were studied in the actual country of origin – immersed in the essence of the words, the language begins to fill the mind and tongue. So it is with colour. Using it everyday, in a great number of ways, will ensure a wholesome comprehension, so that in the end, as any experienced scenic artist can say, it literally becomes second nature.

EXACTLY WHAT IS COLOUR? THE PHYSICS OF COLOUR

The first of all colours is white, although some would not admit that black or white are colours, the first being a source or receiver of colours, and the latter totally deprived of them. But we cannot leave them out, since painting is but an effect of light and shade, that is chiaroscuro, so white is the first then yellow, green, blue and red and finally black. White may be said to represent light without which no colour can be seen.

(Leonardo da Vinci)

Colour exists purely because of light and is carried by light waves. This discovery was made in 1676 by Sir Isaac Newton, whose observations of a triangular piece of glass, known as a prism, showed that when white light was passed through a prism, the light waves bent, breaking up into a spectrum of colours that we recognize as the colours of the rainbow. When these colours were passed back through the prism, they reformed into white light. The phenomenon of a rainbow is exactly what Newton discovered. These colours are: red, orange, yellow, green, blue, indigo and violet. A colour that we then perceive is only possible by the way in which an object has absorbed and reflected light. Hence a blue sky by day, but at night a quite different picture. This perception is made possible by a series of transmissions and processes made by the eye, the brain and the optic nerve.

THE COLOUR WHEEL: THEORIES

Having looked at 'what exactly is colour' we can move onto the theories that have been given to the perception of colour. The first, and without doubt the most important, theorizer of colour was Michel-Eugene Chevreul (1786–1889). A leading chemist of his time working at the great dyeworks of Gobelins Tapestry works in France, Chevreul created the first chromatic colour wheel and established the law of contrasting and complementary colours, after observing the effects that a juxtaposition of colours has on each other. Imagine his fascination on the subject as his work developed from years of observing some of the finest tapestries the world had known at the time.

Here is a description of the colour wheel, based on the one first devised by Chevreul and still in use today, relatively unchanged.

Basically colours are divided into three parts:

* primary colours
* secondary colours
* tertiary colours.

The **primary colours** are:

* red
* yellow
* blue.

All colours can be mixed from primary colours, which are not formed by a mixture of each other.

The **secondary colours** are those that are created from a mixture of two primary colours:

* blue + red = purple
* red + yellow = orange
* blue + yellow = green.

The **tertiary colours** are a mixture of two secondary colours:

* orange + purple = russet
* orange + green = citrine (brownish yellow)
* green + purple = olive.

Complementary colours are the colours that lie opposite each other on the colour wheel. Every colour has a complementary colour, e.g. green is the complementary colour of red. This is shown in the illustration. A helpful way of remembering this is to draw the

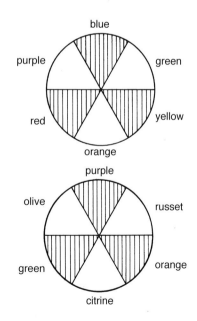

The colour wheel.

wheel for yourself and, quite literally, fill in the correct colours by following the mixtures. One word of advice, however: try to use as pure a colour as possible, as a mix of a pinkish-red with a yellow for a primary mix will result in an orange that will not seem pure.

OPTICAL ILLUSIONS OF COLOUR

Perception of colour is a physical phenomenon that extends further than the average person is aware of, and is intriguing. We can now look briefly at some of these optical illusions as they play an important part in the work of anyone working in colour, and can indeed be used for this very purpose.

* Colours are perceived as being either warm or cool. Blues are termed cool, whereas earth colours are warm. Blues are receding colours. In other words they appear to recede to the eye, as a mountain range appears to be very much in the distance. Artists can use this optical illusion in their work as a way of creating greater distance, and an excellent example of this is to look at the landscapes painted by the Renaissance artists. On the other hand, the colour red appears to be quite stationary, whether it is seen from a distance or close up. However, yellow appears to advance towards the eye. In the world of advertising, this colour can be of great use, as the colour is particularly prominent when sitting on a shelf surrounded by other colours, demanding to be bought!
* The eye requires the presence of the three primary colours at all times when looking at any colour, in whatever form or combination. When it is not there, the eye will create it and cast that which is deficient onto an object nearby. Imagine walking into a red-painted room. On leaving the room, the eyes will create the illusion of the complementary colour green, which will appear on to practically everything!
* The use of juxtaposition of contrasting colours creates an optical vibration. Colours literally appear to shimmer, especially when using the complementary colours. The Pointillist painters, especially Seurat, made great use of this. In certain scenic methods, such as spattering or dottling, which are explained in the following chapter on painting methods, this clever illusion is an effective technique.
* When a light colour is placed next to a dark colour, it appears lighter than it really is. The dark also appears darker.

All these illusions can be of use to artists and designers, and with experience colour is as useful as a tool as the brush itself.

COLOUR TERMINOLOGY

In visual perception a colour is almost never seen as it really is – as it physically is...
(Josef Albers, artist and teacher from the Bauhaus movement)

As remarked on in his innovative teachings on colour, Albers was one of the first teachers of colour to move away from the rather formal theoretical teachings and move towards a more practical level. In this quote from his book *Interaction on Colour*, the words seem quite appropriate for this next explanation on the terminology often equated with colour. Despite there being recognition of colour when seen or named, the true nature of it can be quite different.

Theatre designers, lighting designers and others involved in the more creative production processes, will often be involved in discussions that are likely to confuse an inexperienced scenic artist. Here is an example of the kind of conversations that may occur:

I think that the way in which the backdrop has been painted is correct, but the tone of colour needs to be lighter in order for there to be a strong contrast with the remaining set. You may need to tint the colours further ...

Or:

The success will lie in the way that this gauze will be lit, perhaps a shade lighter for the forest scene?

Therefore, a brief explanation of these terms will aid the analysis of the perceptions of colour:

* **Tone**: this refers to the lightness or darkness of a colour. Hold a coloured object in your hand, and then move it into an area of shadow and the colour is the same, but a darker tone. The same can be said if you were to see the object in greater light than first seen. It is now a lighter tone than before.
* **Contrast**: this word is used when opposites are compared, e.g. when a light colour is juxtaposed next to a dark colour, a contrast is immediately created; or when two complementary colours are placed next to each other, they will create a strong contrast, and it can be quite powerful.
* **Tint**: this is the name used when a colour is made lighter by the addition of white. It can also be used to describe the subtle colour altering of a paint, or glaze, by the addition of a small amount of another colour.
* **Shade**: this has the same meaning as the word tint, except that it refers to the darkening of a colour, usually by the use of black. They both refer to very subtle changes.
* **Saturation**: this describes the intensity of a colour. Certain brands of scenic colour are produced to have a great saturation and intensity, allowing great scope for thinning down (particularly useful for certain types of painting; *see* Chapter 14).

* **Hue**: the properties of a colour that enable the observer to call it red/blue/yellow, etc. This would not include white, black or grey, as they are not accepted as 'colours' in the chromatic, or otherwise described as the scientific, colour sense.

A LOOK AT PAINTS AND DYES

There are no colours, strictly speaking, only colouring materials.
(Jean Dubuffet, modernist artist)

Having looked at the theories, illusions and terminology of colour, it is now time to look at how colour evolved as a painting material.

A brief history of paints and dyes shows us that since the earliest humans, and the discovery of their artworks, there has been a form of painting material. This was found to be natural pigments and dyes. A pigment is basically any substance that is used to give out a colour, whereas a dye is a liquid that contains a colouring material. In order to create different pigments and dyes for artworks in these early times, organic and inorganic substances were used, such as earths, plants, animals and minerals. These could be both rare and difficult to achieve. As centuries passed, and we are still looking at history in BC years, the first use of a synthetically produced pigment was made in Egypt, in the third century BC. This heralded the broadening of the palette of colours, which continued up to, and throughout, the Middle Ages, as seen by the beautiful painted illuminated manuscripts of the time. The invention of optical and atmospheric perspective arrived with the dawning of the Renaissance throughout Europe, and greater experimentation in the Arts meant that colouring materials also underwent further developments in both colour range and methods. By the time the Industrial Revolution had arrived, colour had become a major trade. This was an incredibly important era for colour and paint production, for the likes of Chevreul were working at this time. The nineteenth century was remarkable, with the invention of aniline dyes in 1826 by a German chemist called Otto Unverdorben. This was then patented in England by Henry Pukin and saw the invention of the first ever synthetic dye. The variety of colours became greater than ever, and this development did not slow down into the twentieth century either. The most important development now was to be the invention of the first-ever ready-mixed acrylic paints in 1901 in the laboratory of Otto Rohm in Germany, and later produced for commercial use from the 1930s.

Since Antiquity, colour treatises and their recipes have been written down, from the earliest known writings of Pliny the Elder, through to Joseph Albers in the twentieth century. These very early writings were not only fascinating to read but were, more importantly, a source of invaluable information. For scenic painting this has played an integral role too, as the main painting materials were also pigments and dyes. Little has changed since, and we can now look specifically at this.

All paints are made primarily from pigments, and whether it is an oil colour, water colour or modern-day acrylic or emulsion paint, the difference lies in which 'medium' or 'vehicle' the pigment is suspended in. For example, in oil colour, pigments are suspended in linseed or poppy oil; for watercolour it is gum arabic; and for emulsions and acrylics, it is water. These mixtures then need a 'binder' in order for the mix to adhere to a surface. For scenic paints the binder would originally have been animal glue, known as size, which is also used for priming. The binders now employed in modern scenic paints are plastic polymers, and are man-made (the same ingredient is also used in household or acrylic paints).

A rare number of scenic studios still employ old techniques such as the use of size in paint mixing, and for some individuals the modern equivalents will never achieve the same quality. However, they do have other important qualities: the main one being flexibility, as well as being extremely matt in appearance. The use of plastic polymers in their make-up means that, as these paints are now more flexible, they are far more convenient for travelling and storage, which, in the world of repertory and touring theatre, is vital. This is because soft cloths need to be folded up and placed into travelling baskets, as opposed to the previous storage method of rolling them up onto long wooden battens. A cloth painted in the traditional method of pigment mixed with size is far more likely to have the paint crack than if it is painted in modern flexible colours, due to the way it is stored. The other most obvious reason for this change was the time saved in mixing up colour. The old scenic studios would have had apprentices or labourers, whose job it would have been to make up the glues and mix the colours for the artists. Now of course they are available pre-mixed.

Scenic dyes, known as aniline dyes, are the other main painting material used by scenic artists. These are similar to those used in household dyeing and also for costumiers and prop-makers. Dyes are believed to have been around for as long as pigments, although there is little archaeological evidence for this. Dyed textiles decay faster than the surfaces found to have pigments on, such as cave interiors. However, from the little traces found, archaeologists have discovered that it is highly probable that dyes are indeed as old as pigments. Up until the invention of the synthetic aniline dyes in the nineteenth century, natural substances had been used such as plants, minerals and animals. This invention hailed what was to be a vital moment in the history of dye, with the birth of organic chemistry. However, in more recent times it has been discovered that these dyes carry severe health risks, including being carcinogenic. If used, every health and safety guideline must be employed in the handling and mixing process. This is explained later on in this chapter. However, safe water-based dyes have now been produced, reducing the need to use aniline dyes, and these are available from specialist retailers.

Specialist Scenic Paints, Dyes and Associated Products

Most aspects of colour have now been explained in this chapter and it is time to look at what paints and dyes the twenty-first century scenic artist can expect to use today.

There are quite a few companies that specialize in the manufacture of specialist scenic materials; this includes TV, video, exhibition and film painting too. Companies such as these produce a tremendously wide variety of materials, including:

* **Dry pigments**: the traditional paints used by the scenic artists; they must be stored in a dry place and prepared using an appropriate medium such as glue size or emulsion glaze.
* **Scenic acrylic paints**: these are water-based, matt, non-reflective, flexible, come in a fantastic range of colours and are designed to be used either directly from the pot, as stainers or intended to be diluted. There are also ranges of flame-retardant paints.
* **Specialist water-based paints**: these include metallics, sparklies, fluorescents, as well as colours designed to be seen under UV lighting.
* **Bases and priming products**: a wide range of these are available to cover most surfaces ranging from wood, canvas to metal; they come in both oil- and water-based formulas.

* **Spray paints**: water or oil based, available in matt, gloss, satin or semi-transparent, in a wide variety of colours, as well as metallics and fluorescents.
* **Texture products**: *see* Chapter 15.
* **Emulsion glazes**: for use as a medium with pigments or dyes, or as a type of protective coating for specialist painting such as wood-graining or marbling. They are also used to make glazes by mixing with scenic paints for greater translucency. A note of warning: always do a test-patch first and check the shelf life. These products are notorious for going 'milky' in certain situations, and potentially ruining your artwork.
* **Varnishes and sealants**: a lot of scenic work requires an excellent protective coating, such as floors or certain props. The most popular used in theatre now are the wide range of water-based ones, as they are quick-drying, highly durable and mainly cause no discolouration, unlike their oil-based equivalents. These are excellent and are available in matt, satin and gloss.
* **French enamel varnishes**: these are shellac-based, and are used on props or scenery where transparency is required, such as Perspex/polycarbonate or metallics. Available in a number of different colours and require the appropriate PPE to be worn when used.
* **Aniline dyes and water-based dyes**: aniline dyes come in both water- and spirit-based forms and are available in a number of different colours. They are known to contain hazardous chemicals and therefore the user must wear the appropriate PPE. There are now equivalent safe water-based dyes available that require no medium to be added, which are an excellent alternative.

Most prices are pretty comparable for most of these products, but it is always worth looking around if there is a tight budget. Certain colours with the same name, such as ultra-marine blue, will have different prices from different companies, but the quality or shade may vary tremendously, so it is worth hunting around. The palette of colours available is also extremely wide, with some firms offering a further colour-mixing service to near exact standards. For the beginner, this is not such a good idea for learning, but for matching an existing colour this can be very useful, though also quite expensive. Most of these companies regularly invent new and exciting products that are not only good in the visual sense but also offer greater safety and convenience. It is hard to believe that so many materials previously used were so hazardous to health. Luckily these issues are very much in the minds of manufacturers nowadays, and it is worth being aware of.

For any scenic artist, it is a good idea to have most specialist paint colour charts, catalogues and up-to-date price lists. These companies mostly offer a good delivery service, or alternatively you can buy them off the shelf from either a theatrical chandlers or certain specialist paint suppliers. (A list is given at the end of the book.) These shops not only offer a wide range of materials and equipment, but also give much needed technical advice when required, which is very important.

A question often asked by an inexperienced scenic artist, is about the use of household paints in scenic work. Unless on a very tight budget, this is not a good idea as they are simply not designed with theatre/film/TV in mind. The composition of the paint is different, the palette far more limited and the quality of colour quite different.

BUYING, MIXING AND MATCHING COLOUR

Mixing paints and dyes requires skill and, very importantly, common sense. On any scenic job, if you have spent a quite large amount of money on materials, a quite large portion of this can often be spent on the paints. Therefore, before any buying, it is worth bearing in mind a few considerations. When working out costs, it is a good idea to buy cheaper black and white emulsions for painting things such as stage floors, treads and mixing up your prime, saving your funds for the more valuable items. Look in all old painting cupboards or, if backstage in your theatre, check what stock you may have left. Old pots of scenic paint can often be used as a prime, or as part of a mix or first coat. Most paints will dry out before they are past their sell-by date, and using up old colours can be a useful money saver. Next, try to work out the quantity of paint needed, as near as possible, allowing for touch-ups after. This will get easier with time, and expect to make some misjudgements at the beginning. Working out the square footage or metreage is the easiest way to judge the quantity of paint needed.

When mixing colours it is also important to remember a few points.

* Look at a colour that you want to mix, in order to analyse what colours have gone into it, try to imagine where the colour originated. For example, ask yourself whether a blue is essentially a light or dark blue? Has it got red or green in? Is there a lot of black or white in it? It will be a matter of trial and error at the beginning, but will become increasingly easier as you gain experience.
* Start the mixing process by experimenting with very small amounts of colour. A cleaned-up old plastic white lid is a great way of analysing the colour you are mixing, as it can be frequently rinsed off. Once you are confident of the colours, start mixing with small amounts at a time, adding the colours slowly as you would add essential ingredients to a cookery recipe. Always err on the side of caution, as it is better to be safe than sorry. Mistakes can be expensive.

* When mixing large amounts of colour, make sure you cover and seal the buckets properly when using over a length of time, as they can dry out quickly, especially in hot weather, or mix it all into a clean dustbin, and take out the amount you need as the work progresses. A professional paint mixer on a drill is very useful for bulk mixes, and saves the aching arms for the priming process!

* Try to match the quantity with the correct-size bucket. A large number of small buckets housing the same colour can get confusing, and lead to mistakes.

* Keep a handy bunch of sticks and old brushes around the mixing table specifically for mixing colours. It is too tempting to use your own good brushes at times, and not a good idea. Make sure you also have a good supply of clean water at hand.

* For mixing dry colours, add the water to the pigment slowly, creating a paste and adding water as you require. Some painters swear by using warm water, and often soak dry colours beforehand. The binder, such as an emulsion glaze, is added at the end, and you must always test its sticking quality, preferably on to a piece of the material to be used.

* For mixing scenic pre-mixes, the same treatment is required, except that there are no binders to be added, and cold water is preferable.

* For mixing aniline dyes, protective clothing and equipment must be worn: these are gloves, at all times, and a particle mask. Boiling hot, or very hot water is required to mix these, and the powder is added to the water rather than the other way round. When mixed incorrectly it often becomes immediately lumpy and too difficult to mix further. (The same process is required for mixing metallic powders, the only difference being that these are mixed with cold water.

However, these are also becoming rare, as safer ready mix versions are available on the market.) Only once the mix has cooled sufficiently can the binder be added, otherwise it will curdle. To try to get a good idea of the colour mixed, it is a good idea to check constantly be placing a small brushstroke onto a white surface, such as a plastic lid, before drying off a sample on a fabric.

* You must always test any mixed colours before using them. Do this by painting a small amount on to a surface, preferably a sample of the one that you will be painting onto, and allowing it to dry. Due to time restrictions, this is very often done with a dryer, but be aware of the fact that too much direct heat will change the colour as you will be literally cooking it. A heat gun or hair drier is normally used, and you will need to hold it at a safe distance, moving the heat source as you do to ensure that nothing gets roasted! Do not be tempted to guess the outcome of any mixed paint, as it will always dry a different colour from what you see in the bucket.

* Matching a colour can be surprisingly difficult, especially if there are many layers, or a colour is painted onto a textured surface. A bit of detective work is needed here, and by looking at the back of a model piece you can often see individual colours more clearly. These can often be where the colours have literally dripped behind. Consider also the fact of whether a colour has a matt, satin or glossy finish, as this can also alter the colours.

A look at colour in this way has hopefully inspired the reader to feel quite inspired by it, but also be aware of the fact that, like any great skill, this is something that cannot be learned in a moment. It will take time and effort, but the final effects are so rewarding that it is indeed a journey well worth making.

14 PAINTING

First, the tools of painting will be looked at, covering brushes, spray-guns and the various paint tools, which include stompers/stamps and sponge sticks.

An explanation is then given of the processes of scenic painting, from priming through to the finished effect. This includes various techniques such as lining-in, lay-ins, wet and dry brushing, dottling and stippling, as well as an explanation of the other tools and techniques a scenic artist may use, which include rollers, sponges and masking. The techniques and maintenance of the airless spray-gun are given, as well an explanation of the different effects it is possible to create using this and other spray mechanisms. Tips on specialist painting effects are given, such as basic wood-graining, marbling, glaze work, distressing and gilding.

The old paint frame at Covent Garden.

If a scenic artist were to be asked the main reason why he or she had entered into this particular field of work, they would most probably state that, foremost, it was a great love of painting that led them to this decision, coupled with an interest in theatre or other similarly related field. The fact that a scenic artist is called upon to paint in both large and small scales, and to summon up as many of the many practical and creative resources they have in order to achieve the many required effects, is tremendously appealing to certain like-minded individuals.

BRUSHES

Any brush is made up from three fundamental components:

* **Bristles**: traditionally made from animal hair; the most commonly used are hog bristle, which are mainly imported from China, through to the specialist and lesser used badger, squirrel, ox or horse hair. Variations and qualities of a brush will depend on the softness, length, stiffness and tapering qualities of a hair or bristle, as well as their capacity to quite literally 'hold' the paint whilst in the process of painting. Recent years have seen the manufacturing of brushes made from synthetic fibres, mainly from nylon or polyester. Many of these are excellent, both in value and painting ability.
* **The ferrule**: normally made up from metals such as stainless steel or brass, but traditionally also of leather or string. All bristles or hairs are 'set' into the ferrule by means of an epoxy, and this is connected to the handle. The ferrule comes in a variety of widths, and is either flat or rounded.
* **The handle**: commonly made from a treated or untreated wood or plastic. Designed to be held in a way that is both comfortable for the user, as well as to assist the painting movement in their particular role. For

example, a brush designed to paint large areas, such as a priming brush, has a short, sturdy and strong handle that is easy to grip for the strong regular movements required of the arm, wrist and hand in priming, rather than a stencil brush that is short, rounded and stubby, designed to be held more by the fingers and hand to assist in the less exertive vertical 'dabbing' movements for painting through a stencil.

The brush is an ancient device that is probably the most important tool of all. In a painter's bag there will be a wide variety of different paintbrushes, from the specialist scenic brushes through to conventional decorator's brushes, such as the wide, flat priming brushes through to a fine sable, and all of these will most probably be used at some time. It is important to mention that no two paintbrush collections will be the same, as every painter will

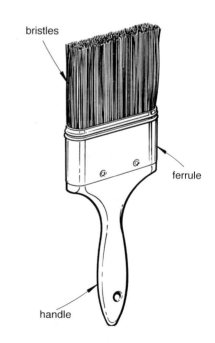

bristles

ferrule

handle

The anatomy of a brush.

have a choice of brushes that are as personal to them as their own wardrobe of clothes; though the basics will all be pretty much the same. The scenic artist will have accumulated these over the years, and it goes without saying that the joy of purchasing new brushes never ceases!

The main brushes used in scenic art, and an explanation of what each may be used for, are listed below.

* **Flat ferruled brushes**: these are made from either bristle or synthetic fibres, and are available in a number of different widths and sizes, and are either angled or straight. These can be used for a number of painting methods, from the priming process through to most other techniques, including glaze work, varnishing, washes, dry brushing, lettering and architectural artwork.

* **Priming brushes**: these are the largest types of brushes a scenic painter will probably use. They are available in 6–9in wide flat ferrules, and are used for priming, 'laying-in' and for covering any large areas that need to be painted.

* **Fitches**: this term refers to the specialist scenic brushes use by scenic artists over the centuries. They come in a variety of sizes, usually from ¼in up to 3in wide and are made up from a long, slender, wooden handle,

long-handled brush

fitches

sash brush

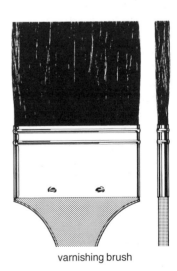

varnishing brush

A selection of scenic art brushes.

opening out into an oval ferrule that is either flattened out or not, making the bristles rounded or flat in the ferrule. They are used for most of the artwork requirements in scenic painting, as opposed to the basic laying-in of flat colour.

* **Sash brushes**: this term derives from a brush originally used in the decorating trade for painting sash window frames. The bristles are trimmed at an angle all round, unlike a fitch, and are set on a long handle with either a round or oval ferrule. They have a number of uses, but are particularly good for painting any sorts of line.

* **Liners**: this term refers to a brush used for painting any lines, either straight or curved, and can be bought as a scenic fitch brush or as a traditional decorator's sash or liner brush. They are designed to hold the paint in such a way that the 'line' is completed as uniformly as possible.

* **Long-handled brushes**: these are mainly used for floor painting. Some are available as separate detachable long handles, which are designed to attach to a variety of sizes of heads. Alternatively, any shaped brush can be attached to a suitable pole when required. Extendable poles are also available and are ideal for touching up scenery once it has been fitted up on stage.

Specialist Painting Brushes

* **Wood-grainers**: these are made from stiffer bristles, which help to create a grainy look to the glaze by spreading it into finely spaced lines.

* **Over-grainers**: a row of brushes incorporated into one brush to help create wider-spaced grain lines in wood-graining.

* **Draggers**: these are used without glaze on as their dryness helps to break up the glaze to create good grainy effects in wood-graining.

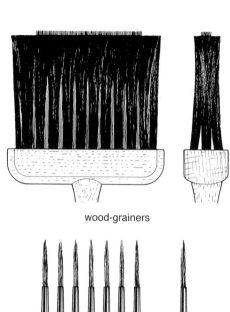

wood-grainers

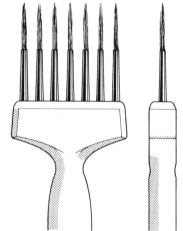

pencil over-grainers

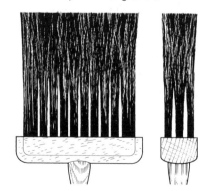

draggers

(Above and opposite page) A selection of the more specialist brushes.

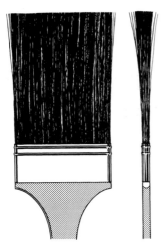

floggers

* **Floggers**: these have very long bristles that are used to create the background to wood, using a flicking action on the glaze – hence the name of the brush.
* **Stipplers**: the action of these brushes is to soften colour by evenly distributing the wet paint. They can produce anything from fine freckles to a soft mottling in wood-graining.
* **Mottlers**: these are for creating highlights and shades in wood.
* **Stencil brushes**: these are short, stubby brushes, designed to apply the paint by a dabbing action.
* **Softeners**: these are made from a soft hair, such as badger, and are simply for softening any paint effects.
* **Sign-writer's brushes**: these are made from long, soft, animal hairs such as squirrel and are designed to hold a lot of paint.

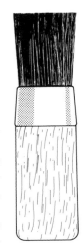

stencil brush

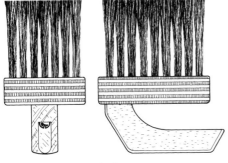

stipplers

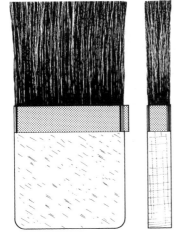

mottlers

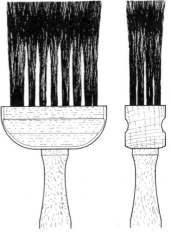

softeners

This shows a good basic collection of brushes that a scenic artist uses, illustrating the wide variety of types and sizes.

Where to Obtain Brushes

For anyone wanting to start in a career in scenic art, it is obviously important to have a good collection of brushes. However, when funds are low, start with a collection of the absolute basics, as listed here:

* a selection of decorator's brushes, in a variety of sizes ranging from 22mm (1in) up to at least 100mm (4in);
* a priming brush, such as a decorator's wall brush – preferably 125–150mm (5–6in) wide;
* a selection of scenic fitches, ranging from 10mm (½in) through to 50mm (2in); there

A cloth bag is ideal for carrying your brushes.

are sets available through specialist suppliers and are worth the initial investment, if maintained well, as they should last a lifetime;
* a dusting-off brush, used for clearing any surface you are about to paint.

All painter/decorator brushes are available from good DIY stores, who stock a wide collection of brushes for specialist painting methods. Decorator brushes, specialist brushes and scenic brushes are available from theatrical chandlers, and are listed at the end of the book. The final item you need is to buy a paintbrush bag to transport all your brushes. Make sure that the bag you buy is made of a breathable material, as all brushes containing any moisture will rot unless allowed to breathe properly.

TOOLS FOR PAINTING

Basically, anything goes as concerns scenic painting, and if a scenic artist is confronted with an effect to create that needs the invention of some obscure tool not known to anyone else, then so be it. Do not feel afraid of trying anything – within reason, of course! There are, however, a number of tools that are particularly handy and these can now be looked at.

Stompers on a paint tray.

Stompers

These are sometimes known as stamps, and are a wonderful way of achieving repeat patterns and designs, such as foliage. To make one you will need to take an offcut of plywoood, chosen to be a size slightly larger than the image you are re-creating, and use a foam rubber that is a good 25–75mm (1–3in) thick. Cut out your design using a sharp knife or blade, and stick this on to the plywood base using a good non-invasive glue. You will need a handle on the top of the stamp, as well as an indication of which direction your design is facing. Always test the stomper before using, making any necessary alterations before you use it on the actual piece of scenery. When using a tool like this you should treat it in the same way as any painting tool, allowing freedom in your movements, so that the impressions made are not too uniform. This can be achieved by changing the pressure with which you press, as well as tilting it to create further variations.

Sponge Sticks

These are a delight when wanting to achieve a certain line or mark that no brush could ever achieve. They allow for extremely swift arm movements and are ideal for floor painting. They can be made up in all sizes. All that is needed is a pole, bamboo or other such handle, a piece of foam rubber cut into a rectangular block, glue and a piece of string. First, make an incision of about 25–75mm (1–3in) exactly in the centre at one end of the foam rubber. Put some non-invasive glue on this and stick your pole into the incision. Tie the string very tightly around the foam, about 23mm (1in) from the bottom. Now cut the top half of the foam into the required shape, as shown in the photograph overleaf, A variety of shapes and sizes can be created.

A variety of marks can be made by sponge sticks.

Rollers

Foam rollers can be cut into any shape and used as a painting tool. Rollers are now available in varying sizes, which is really useful. Any design can be created: from straight lines, leaves or just simply a 'textured' effect, as shown. As with stompers, test them first and make any necessary adjustments. To create the shapes, a variety of methods can be used, such as a sharp blade, a pair of pliers, a very hot piece of metal or even fingers (when melting foam, the correct PPE must be worn as toxic fumes are given off).

(Top right) Sponge sticks and rollers.
(Main picture) Here a photocopy grainy effect was required, and only rollers were used in the painting to re-create this feel.
(Inset) Detail.

*Here an effective leafy
effect is required.*

Sponges

Any sponges can be used from the soft and exquisite natural sponges to the man-made varieties. If you ever travel to Greece, it is worth buying your sponges there as they are much cheaper than from any art suppliers. Sponges are a great tool for softening, blending, dabbing on or off, as well as for cleaning up your work.

(Inset) Sponges will create great effects.
(Main picture) An example of sponge work is seen on this tree and landscape.

Rags

A selection of rags are always useful, and never throw away any old bits of fabric if they can be used elsewhere. Rags can be dipped into paint and used to create the well-known rag-rolling effects, as well as used to dab or rub off paint for alternative effects.

CARE AND MAINTENANCE OF ALL PAINTING TOOLS

The care and maintenance of all painting tools is of the utmost importance. A painter's brush collection will have amounted to a considerable sum of money spent over the years, as well as taking on the characteristics of the individual. Most painters would agree that nothing could replace it. You must, therefore, be diligent in cleaning brushes after use, using warm soapy water that is not too hot, and testing that there is no more paint left in by flicking the 'cleaned ' brush over your hand to check that the water runs clean. Mould each set of bristles back into shape gently with by hand and leave them to dry out in the open, preferably with the bristles facing downwards so that all the water runs out. A brush that is left dirty will be ruined when the paint dries, and will rot if left in water too long or left to dry in an airless space, such as a plastic toolbox. This rule applies to rollers, sponges and any other tool that a painter may have used.

STARTING THE PAINTING PROCESSES

In this section, the order of the painting process is explained. Of course there may be designs that need more or less of any one of these processes, but this will give the reader an overview of what to expect. Spend a while getting organized, with a table set up with everything needed laid out on to it. This will include all the colours required, clean buckets, sieves for any spray work, brushes and any other appropriate painting tools (this is discussed further in this chapter), the model pieces and any appropriate references close to hand. For the palette, a handy tip is to use either an old piece of white formica or clean plastic paint tops. You are now ready to start.

The Lining-In Process

'Lining-in', though not used by all scenic painters, is highly recommended for the following reasons.

* It is a process by which your drawing, prior to being primed, is literally inked-in using either a weak mix of dye or paint, preferably in one of the darker earth colours.
* It is a way of 'cleaning' up the drawing process by eliminating any unwanted lines, as well as enabling a prime to be painted over the top; the drawing is not lost in this process.
* This process is ideal for designs that require more complex drawing, or where there may be a risk of losing a drawing in subsequent priming or painting.

The Priming Process

This has been described in Chapter 11, but it is important to understand the logical order of all scenic processes. A tip about priming is that it does not necessarily have to be white. If you look at the design, and it happens to be a lovely sky cloth, then the prime can be a pale blue, or a traditional landscape is complemented well by a light yellow ochre prime.

The Lay-In

Not in this case a lazy Sunday morning pastime, but the first use of colour on a piece of scenery or cloth. Referring to the model reference, the entire surface should be covered, blocking in all the main areas, using a darker tone for the darker areas, such as any shadows, and similarly putting lighter tones where there are the lighter areas. Areas needing a 'textured paint' effect can be painted-in quite freely, and any brush strokes made at this point will lay the foundations for the rest of the painting and are used as a guide in many cases, such as a 'grainy' feel to an area that will become wood. It is important that there should be no attempt at doing any of the finer or detailed work at this point. The 'lay-in' will allow the painter to get a much better idea of how the picture is developing as a 'whole', rather than fragmented.

Building Up the Picture

This refers, quite literally, to building up an image using appropriate colours, paint textures and any finer detailing needed to bring it to a point of near completion. With referral to the model piece, as opposed to copying brush stroke for brush stroke, the painter allows the work to take on his or her personal interpretation. Keep stepping back from the work, either looking at it from a height or distance, and keeping in mind that all scenic work is designed to be viewed as such.

This illustrates the sequential build-up of a painting of an icon, illustrating the lining-in, the lay-in, and gradual build-up to the finished piece (overleaf).

The finished piece.

Highlights and Shadows

Knowing when a painting is finished is difficult; it is important not to over-paint, as this can spoil any effect. However, getting to a point where you are highlighting the lightest points and deepening any shadows, you know that you are not far off. Both of these processes must be done with a key word, 'subtlety', unless of course you are working on a pantomime set, but that would require another book. When you feel you are nearly there, look at the work through half-closed eyes, standing at a distance from it, as this will help to see any inconsistencies, as well as seeing the work more clearly.

PAINTING TECHNIQUES WITH BRUSHES

There are many different ways of using paint-brushes, and with time and practice you will soon become accustomed to each movement, as a child does when learning to ride a bicycle. Here is a selection of the main scene-painting techniques:

* **Dry brushing**: any flat ferruled brush is ideal, and very little paint will be required on the brush. It is ideal for highlighting and, particularly, for emphasizing any three-dimensional textures. Having dipped the brush into the paint, work most of it off on to a cloth or other nearby surface, before starting to paint. Using a very light touch at first and, holding the brush in a position where it is very close to the texture, use a light dragging movement in one direction, as opposed to back and forth.

The Designer's Input

It is at this point that, in both an amateur as well as professional capacity, the designer may or may not make an appearance to view the work. Very rarely will a designer like to see the work once on stage, and normally it is viewed whilst still in the workshops. Expect criticism, and allow for adjustments in whatever capacity, and understand that even this can change once the whole set is seen on stage and under full stage lighting. It is at this point that one is made constantly aware of the combination of skills that make up a stage set, and this can be both a humbling, as well as an exhilarating, experience.

Dry brushing.

* **Blending**: is where two colours are blended subtly; it is done by introducing a second colour in with the first and really working the brush to literally mix the two together, as more of the second colour is gently introduced until the first is left behind.
* **Painting lines**: this can be done using a straight edge (on a stick, for floor painting, or handle, for upright painting). Make sure

Blending.

the straight edge is regularly wiped clean of any excess paint to avoid putting drips on to the painted surface.

* **Working with thin washes**: this is a lovely way of re-creating water-colour effects, or building up a colour through means of layers. A touch of an emulsion glaze can be added to the paint mix, which will add greater lustre to the work. This method is better for floor painting, though it can be done vertically if done with great care, and not allowing there to be too much paint on the brush. Most brushes can be used for this method.
* **Spattering**: this is for creating or adding a painted 'texture' to any paintwork by means of lots of dots of paint spattered off a loaded brush of paint. It is one of the most commonly used scenic techniques. A wide brush, such as a 100–180mm (4–7in) wide flat

This image shows how thin washes can be used to re-create the effect of watercolour.

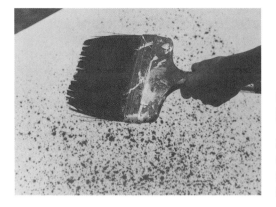

Spattering.

by the action of 'dabbing' at the paint with either a stippling brush, or other type of brush, as opposed to drawing the brush up or down on a surface.

Curious Devices Used in Scenic Painting

In this section some of the handy devices are explained that a scenic artist may use to create a certain effect that neither simply a brush-stroke nor roller could create on its own.

ferruled brush is needed, or a decorator's block brush. This is then dipped into the paint and, having knocked off any excess paint on to the side of the bucket, used with a flicking action over the surface to be spattered, holding the brush horizontally over the surface being painted. If your lower arm muscles are not in pain the following day, then you are not doing this correctly!

* **Stippling**: this refers to the method of softening colours or glazes, or distributing them

Masking
This refers to the way in which certain areas can be covered up whilst another is being painted or textured. This can be done by a number of different ways, such as using cut-out polythene, old bits of cardboard, newspaper, micafil or quite simply masking tape. Take, for example, a picture with an horizon line of high-rise buildings set against a sprayed sunset sky. The easiest way of achieving a crisp and neat division between the two is to cover up one entire section whilst working on the other, then reversing the process, and in that way you will create the desired effect. A word of warning:

Areas can be protected with masking tape whilst others are being painted.

take great care in not getting the masking too wet with paint that it soaks through, and likewise take care when removing any polythene when working on the floor, as the paint will sit in pools on the surface.

Stencils

In Chapter 12, the method of making stencils was described, and when it comes to painting with them, it is important to stick to a few rules to avoid any problems:

* make sure the alignment is always correct before committing yourself to any painting;
* make sure that the paint is quite thick, otherwise it will run under the edges;
* choose a brush that suits the scale of the job: stencil brushes are all very well for smaller designs, but are mainly intended for household interiors, as opposed to the scale of scenic work – using a sponge roller through a stencil is also a way of creating a lovely effect;
* once all the painting has been done, you are now free to paint in the little areas that were left blank from the stencil 'ties'.

SPRAY-PAINTING TECHNIQUES

First of all it is important to look at the different mechanisms with which paint can be sprayed.

* **Airless spray-guns**: these send the paint directly through the hose under great pressure and are used a lot in studios that want to paint large flat areas, and quickly!
* **Gravity feed-guns**: these use compressed air sent through the hose to force out the paint. They are most commonly used in the scenic trade. They come in a variety of qualities and sizes, and are well worth the investment for any one wishing to take up scenic art as a full-time career.
* **Hand-held misters**: otherwise known as garden sprayers, these are ideal for smaller jobs, breaking down a prop or small ser where a gravity feed-gun is not available.
* **Pump sprayer**: it was one of these beauties, introduced into scenic art in the nineteenth century, that saw the first ever spray work. It is a tough and dependable tool, which is often used for fire-proofing, as well as for painting.

To re-create an 'aged' texture to the background of this image, paint was sprayed over micafil (vermiculite), which acted as a masking.

✳ **Artist's diffuser**: this nifty little tool is ideal for any touch-up work on stage, or for ageing and breaking down props and smaller pieces of scenery.

Learning to use any spray technique just needs time and practice and, once this has been mastered, you are free to create wonderful effects that are as expressive as any other method of painting. For the techniques about to be explained, a gravity feed-gun is used for the description. Here are a few tips:

✳ First, you need to understand that, for any spray technique, it is the movement of the whole arm and body that is used, and not just the hand and arm, as one would imagine.

✳ When working on the floor, the painter's posture is important, in order not to get a stoop or backache, and in doing this the painter should stand as upright as possible.

✳ Always sieve your paint mix before using the gun, as the smallest of particles can block it, therefore wasting precious time.

✳ Regularly check for any blockages in any of the air holes and, if blocked, stick a pin into them to remove the obstruction.

✳ Always make sure that the hose leading to the gun is free of any kinks, as these will obviously affect the air supply and, subsequently, the spray that is released.

✳ Wear the appropriate PPE when doing a lot of spray work.

Get to Know Your Spray-Gun

In order to get to know a spray-gun, it is a good idea to be able to take it apart and put it back together with your eyes closed. This can be done in only a minute, and helps the scenic artist understand the way in which it works, and also enables them to take it apart swiftly when required. For example, whenever there are blockages, which there often are at the most inconvenient times, and when speed and dexterity are called for. The care and maintenance of all such equipment is vital, and cleaning after any paintwork has been done is imperative. Every so often it is a good idea to take a spray-gun apart and give each component an especially good clean. There are certain specialist 'gun' cleaners available, but care must be taken when using these as they are toxic. All PPE should be worn. A dab of petroleum jelly on any of the screw fittings of your gun will also help to preserve it.

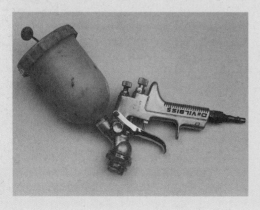 

How Thick Should the Paint Be?

A question often asked is how thick or thin a mix of paint should be for any of the processes described. Basically, there are no prescribed formulas or hard and fast rules, but with time and experience you will begin to know exactly how each job will determine this question, and in the meantime any mistakes must all be considered as a lesson learnt.

Below, some spray techniques are described.

Creating a Flat Colour with Spray

Creating a flat colour with a spray can never be done in one go: it is necessary to build up the layers until the whole surface appears even. The main aim is to be as consistent as possible, working in a methodical manner right across the surface. It is a good idea to practise on a piece of wood, the floor or canvas to get the rhythm, and gain confidence.

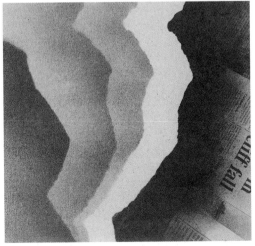

(Above right) Wear the appropriate PPE when doing a lot of spraying.
(Above) Creating a flat colour with spray.

Here a piece of newspaper is used for effective spray techniques.

161

Here dottle was used in order to re-create the grainy effect of a photograph in a production of Troilus and Cressida *at RADA, designed by Julie Nelson, directed by Robin Midgely.*

Masking with Spray

This can either be done with stencils, masking as mentioned earlier in this chapter, or with a simple piece of wood or even torn paper, depending entirely on the effect required.

Spray-gun Dottle

By varying the position of the cap that reduces the air flow to the paint, and subsequently reducing or increasing the strength of the vacuum in the gun, a variation of paint effects are produced. Not too dissimilar to the technique of spattering, mentioned earlier in brush techniques, 'dottling' produces a more uniform and even size of paint spot on to the surface. Turning the cap, more or less, can vary the size of paint spots, and this is a really useful technique.

Creating a Gradation with Spray

Working in the same method as with a flat colour, another colour is introduced in a methodical and even way; this also requires a number of layers of careful spraying in order to achieve an excellent gradation. Having introduced another colour, it may be necessary to bring back a little of the original colour at the end in order to even out the final effect, and soften the overlap (*see* photograph right).

This illustrates a gradation of spray.

WOOD-GRAINING

There are a few ways of achieving a scenic, painted-wood effect, either with texture, as described in the following chapter, or by using specialist wood-graining tools and brushes. The example given uses specialist tools and brushes to give a more realistic effect, but first considers the paints to use. The example uses scenic water-based paints; most professional wood-grainers, outside of theatre, use mainly oil-based paints.

Paints

You will need:

* prime, a minimum of two coats, a pale background colour to the required wood;
* about two or three colours, known as glazes, made up from emulsion glazes and colour;
* sealant or varnish to seal and enhance the work.

Any wood-graining needs a good prime whether working on a canvas or on wood. On a wooden surface, make sure that the prep work has been done extremely well. The prime needs to be tinted with colour. Look at the reference you are simulating and decide what is the palest colour you can see, such as a creamy colour for a pine, or pinkish colour for a mahogany. Ideally, you should then coat the prime with a layer of emulsion glaze, either gloss or matt. This will help the colours glide on more smoothly. Scenic emulsions and dry pigments can both be used, and most scenic artists have their personal preferences. You rarely need more than two or three colours, and these will be:

* a mid-tone for creating the background;
* a darker colour for creating the grain of the wood;
* an optional third glaze for further colouring the wood, such as a darker wood needing more intensity or ageing.

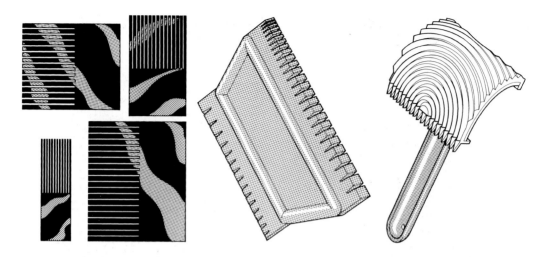

Here are some specialist tools used for wood-graining. These include metal graining combs, rubber combs and a heart grainer.

When mixing colours for wood-graining, or indeed marbling, emulsion glazes or vinyl-based scumble glazes are normally used. These help to re-create the translucency of these natural materials. Always test colours before using them, and do this by priming a sizeable sample board using the same processes and colours for the actual scenery to be painted.

Specialist Wood-Graining Tools

The tools and brushes used to 'create' a painted wood effect are:

* graining combs;
* rubber rocker heart grainers;
* the brushes described in the previous section on specialist brushes.

All of these are the tools of the professional wood-grainer, but are also used in the scenic trade to achieve realistic wood-graining for props, or perhaps scenery that will be viewed at close quarters.

Technique for a Basic Wood-Grain

This example gives a very basic technique for a wood-grain. Designers will normally have a very good idea of the exact wood they require and it is often up to the scenic artist to come up with a reference. A real one is always helpful!

You will need to work quickly as glazes dry quickly, and cannot be overworked. Working on a smooth and well-primed surface, use a flat ferruled brush to lay in the first glaze as evenly as possible, and only work on a limited area at a time as the glaze will dry too quickly otherwise. Texturing to resemble the distinctive background of wood can be achieved by gently using a brush such as a flogger along the length of the glaze to break it up. When this has dried, the next glaze can be laid in and a rocker applied using a gentle rolling movement as it is pulled through the glaze: this will create the distinctive grain of the wood. Any lines can be softened by gently using a dragger in one direction, and a final glaze can be applied using a grainer. To finish the effect, a coating of glaze is required in a gloss, matt or satin, in order to accentuate the colours and protect the work.

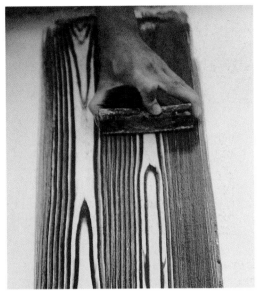

Laying on the glaze, using a flat ferruled brush. The distinctive characteristics of wood can already be seen by the brush's bristles.

Here a rocker grainer is used to re-create the very distinctive grain of wood.

Here a sample of wood graining shows how effective it can be.

A Cheaper Alternative

When funds are not available to buy a set of wood-graining brushes and tools, there are simpler methods! Here are some alternatives.

* A basic selection of decorating brushes can be used for laying-in the glazes as well as any softening needed, but for the more wood-like effects, a brush that has become rather old with its bristles splayed is ideal for achieving the grain, as well as clumping and tying the bristles of a standard flat ferruled brush together for achieving wider-spaced grain.
* A comb can be made out of a piece of stiff plastic, such as a those on a paint bucket.
* The end of a piece of bamboo dipped in paint is a good method for creating the distinctive 'knots' in a piece of wood – this will produce a broader and more 'scenic' style of wood, but just as challenging to achieve!

MARBLING

A helpful method when painting marble is to try and get some off-cuts and really look at them to understand the depth and translucency that is so inherent in this beautiful material. To achieve this in a simple painted way, an effective method is to work in a series of layers, laying colour on colour, and using water and spattering, which help to mimic the natural shapes in marble. As the liquid pools, add further dabs of colour that behave in a wonderfully organic manner and help the painting look more realistic. Use a rag or sponge to remove any paint you do not want. Any veining can be done with a brush, but make sure to observe the true pattern of these as they weave their way through the material. If working on an upright piece, this organic feel can be achieved by means of dry brushing and blending of colours, working up the layers in the same way. A rag or sponge is also needed here, as the removal of any paint can be as important as the application of it. A swan's feather is optional, but they are normally used for smaller pieces of work, and are not ideal for any large-scale work. The final effect to a good marble is to glaze it well in order to enhance its translucency.

AGEING AND DISTRESSING

A part of any scenic artist's job is to age, breakdown or distress any part of a set or prop. It is a way of softening the 'newness' of it, as well as actually making a set look visibly worn. When lit, colours often appear tonally lighter than in

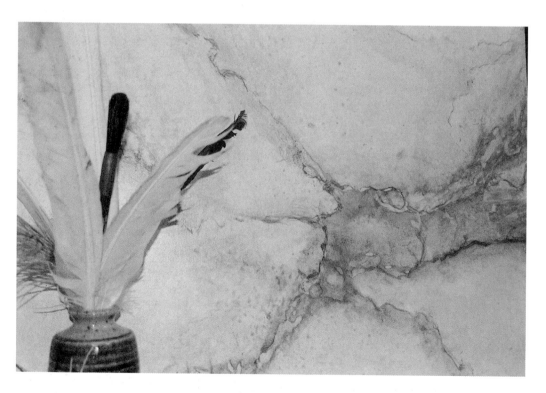

Marbling.

reality, so the job of breaking down is very important. This can mean using tools such as hammers, blow torches, sand-blasting, axes, sand-paper and files, or simply with paint, re-creating rust, age, even decay. Indeed both will often be employed. An excellent colour to use is 'van dyke crystals', a dye that is the traditional way of breaking down scenery used in theatre (prepare using the same method as all aniline water-based dyes). Props, such as upholstered furniture, can be broken down using a light spray of van dyke through a piece of old lace, and an artist's diffuser is ideal for onstage paintcalls when breaking down smaller pieces, such as picture mounts or china.

Gilding

A highly effective method for making both props or parts of any painting that much more luxurious, is to gild. This is not using the real materials, but a far cheaper and just as effective alternative used in theatre, known as Dutch metal and the newer foil leaf. This is available from theatrical as well as specialist decorative paint suppliers. Dutch metal is available as gold, silver and copper, and comes in loose leaf or transfer form, as small squares made up into books. Metallic-foil leaf comes in a greater variety of colours, and has the advantage of coming in actual rolls, as well as being a good width.

Gilding with Dutch metal produces stunning effects.

Preparation work is to paint your surface with an appropriate emulsion colour, traditionally red oxide for gold and grey for silver. Yellow ochre is also widely used for golds and coppers too. Then, preferably using a water-based size painted on to the appropriate areas, wait until this has become 'tacky' before applying the metals. Once pressed into place, a light rubbing with fingers on to the transfers will help to secure them, before lifting off either the paper or plastic backing. Use an extremely soft brush, such as a badger-haired one, for the loose leaf. To protect any gilding, varnishes or specialist waxes can be used. However, make sure you sample a product first as some brands repel the metal. To paint on to any gilding, FEVs can be used, either manually or by spray, and their translucency ensures that the metals retain their sparkle.

There are more effective and highly specialized scenic painting techniques than those given here, but any serious enthusiast will appreciate that, once these basics are grasped, there will be plenty of time to learn even more.

Gilding on an icon.

15 TEXTURES

In this chapter the use of textures in scenic art is explained. The three main types of techniques used in scenic art are: wet textures; the application of pre-moulds and vacforms; and the techniques of basic carving and applied texturing. A list of the tools and appropriate materials is given for all these, as well as examples of each technique to illustrate their uses. Where specialized tools or materials are described and listed, cheaper and more economical alternatives are given wherever possible.

Textures play an extremely important role in theatre design. A designer may wish to create a sense of strong realism or, quite simply, use both visual and tactile qualities of textures as an expression on their own. A collaboration of shapes, colours and textures are all part of the scheme used by a designer to portray a personal vision. Not only does an audience get to appreciate these effects, but also, for scenic artists and lighting designers alike, a textured set can be tremendously satisfying to work on. A beautifully textured set, whether it has had the techniques of carving or rustic plaster walls applied, will literally be brought to life by lighting, as the three-dimensional qualities will be brought into play by the use of light and shadows. It is important to learn how to apply these skills well, and not to think of this job as merely re-enacting the age-old Italian trattoria! Learning how to use the wide variety of textures will broaden any creative person's imagination, as the potential of this highly tactile medium is realized. It can be a pleasure, not only to apply textures but, having finished this process, there is the final satisfaction of the painting process. Here the results of all your hard work will be revealed!

Having looked at a design, a scenic artist may well have to ask themselves certain questions concerning a textured set. After analysing a design it may well be that there are a number of alternatives available to produce a given texture, e.g. a rustic grainy wood effect. This could be achieved in a number of ways:

* real wood, perhaps sand-blasted and blow-torched;
* wet texture applied and 'wood-grained';
* a vacform mould;
* polystyrene carved to look like wood.

Vacforms and Pre-Moulds

Vacform is a process by which plastic sheets are heated, causing them to become malleable. They are then pulled into place by a vacuuming process on to a positive heat-resistant mould. On cooling, the new shape has become permanent. The advantages of this are that many copies can be made of any design. Pre-moulds are usually made from plaster or polyresins or PVC. Like vacforms they are made from casts and are, therefore, available as a choice of designs directly through theatrical prop suppliers. A cheaper alternative, for architectural mouldings say, is to buy them directly from a DIY home store, but you will not have such a wide choice.

The decision will lie ultimately in a number of factors. These could be either the scenic artist's or the designer's personal preference, the results of sampling, or quite simply the budget.

Different Ways of Texturing

Textures can pretty much be divided into three main categories:

* textures that are wet on application: these include Artex and Idenden;
* textures that are pre-moulded: these include vacforms and pre-cast moulds;
* textures that are created by carving or application: these include polystyrene, sponge, foams and fabrics.

TOOLS NEEDED FOR TEXTURING

Here is a general list of the tools you will need for texturing:

* **a selection of mixing buckets** in a variety of sizes for wet texture (for really large amounts, a clean plastic dustbin is ideal);
* **paint-mixing drill** is really useful for mixing up large quantities of textures: alternatively make a device called a plunger;
* **plenty of polythene** as most forms of texturing can be a very messy business;
* **air texture gun,** used with an air compressor, and available from specialist theatrical chandlers (*see* Useful Addresses); sounds rather expensive but they are surprisingly good value, and excellent for a variety of effects, which are explained below;
* **trowels, filling and scraper knives**: anything can be used to apply textures (hands included);
* **all appropriate PPE**, including clothing, shoes, rubber gloves and masks;
* **a selection of sharp knives** for carving, old kitchen ones will do;
* **staple gun** for attaching pre-moulded

textures, such as vacform;
* **rollers**: any type can be used to apply texture, as well as those designed specifically for this task;
* **sponges**: a choice of decorator's or natural sponges is a good way of applying wet textures;
* **wood-graining tools**: for creating three-dimensional wood effects;
* **wire brushes** are ideal for removing polystyrene, as well as using on wood.

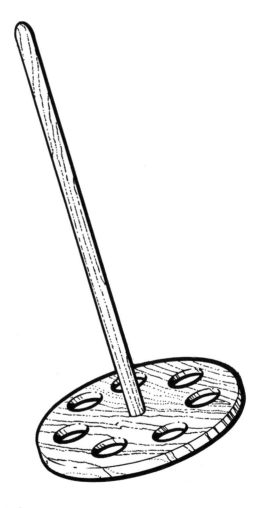

A plunger.

(Right) An air texture gun. (Below right) Wet textures create a variety of surfaces that are ideal for subsequent painting and lighting.

WET TEXTURES

Textures that are wet on application are used for re-creating effects such as plaster walls, wood or barks, various stone effects, brickwork and frescoes. This method can be tremendously versatile as it is mixed thickly or thinly, can be applied manually or used in a texture spray-gun, and will adhere to most soft and hard surfaces.

There are two ways of using wet textures: either by using brand-name, specialist, scenic, ready mixed 'textures', such as Idenden; or by using conventional dry powders, such as Artex, and Toupret.

Once mixed, other materials can be added, such as sawdust, barks, sand, micafil and colour for tinting. Most textures will intermix, creating a far broader range of textures. Standard builders' merchants and good DIY stores stock their own brands of pre-mix textured paints, which can be cheaper in some cases, and just as good (micafil/vermiculite is a naturally occurring inert fire-proof material).

171

The choice of texture will depend on various factors, such as budget, the need for flexibility or simply a personal choice. For those who are inexperienced in textures, it is a good idea to experiment with a few, as they all have quite different qualities, such as:

* flexibility, which can mean that a texture is too difficult to sand down;
* absorbency and non-absorbency will affect the type of painting required (e.g. a highly absorbent texture will soak up paint immediately and could appear too patchy), it all depends on the effect required and the type of primer used, or not.

How to Mix Wet Textures

Mixing wet textures is not only a messy business but, more importantly, it is a health and safety issue. The mixing of such fine particles can be an irritant and, therefore, all necessary precautions should be taken. As mentioned in Chapter 3, a room set aside for mixing is ideal, but where this is not possible, ensure that plenty of polythene is laid out and a particle mask is worn, as well as wearing plastic gloves when directly handling the powders. It is for this reason that specialist companies are developing less potentially harmful ready-mixed textures, which are normally used direct from the bucket and require little or no preparation.

For dry powders, use an appropriately sized bucket (or dustbin) for the estimated amounts needed and mix the powders with slightly warm water. When mixing Artex, you ideally need to pre-soak the powder and water together at least an hour before mixing properly, as this helps reduce the possibility of lumps forming. Pour the powder on to the water.

Specialist, scenic, ready-mixed textures have now been developed into materials that, following application, will dry to a hard enough surface to be sanded, carved or smoothed. This is recommended for creating textures such as bark or stone, and is therefore tough enough to be used on floors (although a good sealant is vital).

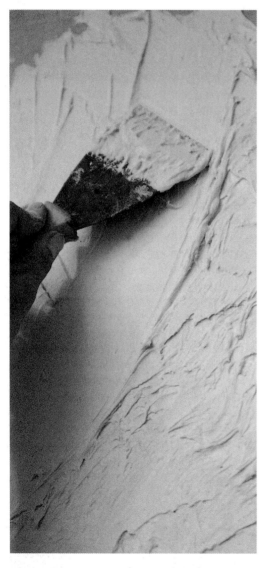

Applying wet textures.

WAYS OF APPLYING TEXTURE

Basically all of the textures can be applied with anything, e.g. a texture spray-gun, piece of wood, a roller, a brush, a sponge or even hands! Consider the desired effect and decide from there. Below are two examples as illustration:

* A grainy piece of old wood. This requires a grainer, and a thickish mix of texture (e.g. the consistency of a cake mix). Idenden is ideal for this purpose, slightly thinned down with water and tinted with a bit of a yellowy earth colour. Having prepared the surface correctly (*see* Chapter 11), first brush on the texture with a paintbrush then, quite quickly, so that it does not dry too rapidly, draw the grainer through the mix, rocking the grainer as you move it. Clean off any excess before starting another piece. Leave to dry before painting. This applies to all textures.

This sequence (1–3) shows how a flat surface of real wood can become far more three-dimensional using textures.

This design, by Janey Gardiner for Saturday, Sunday, Monday, *a RADA production, directed by Joseph Blatchley, shows how a naturalistic effect can be created of an old Italian kitchen using Artex and thin washes of colour onto the unprimed raw surface.*

✳ An old plaster wall. Artex looks particularly good as a plaster effect and can be later painted on to directly with or without prime. This helps to re-create a beautiful surface for authentic painted effects such as colour washes and frescoes. The surface to which the texture is to be applied needs to be particularly well sealed before applying the texture. This is especially so for a wood base. Either shellac-based ones or a thinned-out solution of PVA will do (*see* Chapter 11). It is also a good idea to add an extra large dollop of PVA glue to the texture mix as an added safety measure for an excellent adhesion. Trowel the texture on to the surface with similar movements to that of a plasterer, using a separate bucket of clean water to dip your trowel into and smooth off. This will help to create a lovely surface, where any inconsistencies add further character!

Texture Guns

Another method of applying these wet textures is by an air texture gun. Here are some important points:

✳ Be diligent in protecting any surrounding items that are not required to be sprayed: this includes the floor, the electrical switches on the walls and any model pieces left lying around!

174

* After using a texture spray-gun, be sure to clean it out thoroughly soon after finishing: take it apart completely and wash in very hot soapy water. If this is not done, the next user will have a terrible job trying to remove dried out hardened texture, and it could be you!
* Using masking tape and polythene/newspaper, make sure that any part of scenery that is not required to be sprayed is covered up. The force of this tool is very strong and the texture can permeate the smallest chinks left uncovered.
* In mixing up texture for the gun, make sure the consistency is absolutely right: too thick and it will not come out of the nozzle; too thin and it will create a sloppy mess on the surfaces.
* Using a spray texture gun is a fast, efficient and effective way of creating some excellent textures.

Air texture guns are ideal for effects such as stone for both walls and floors, as well as an economical way of creating brickwork. Two examples of these methods are given here.

This production photo of Accrington Pals, *designed by Neil Irish and directed by Graham Watts, shows the use of a textured floor using a texture gun.*

Stone Slab Floor

To create this effect, either draw out the correct-sized slabs directly on to the floor (which will most probably come from the carpentry workshop in 8ft by 4ft sheets of ply or hardboard) or have them delivered as pre-cut individual pieces. Depending on the amount of space available in the workshop, either lay out the whole floor or, if working in a constricted space, work on a few at a time. Mix up enough texture to cover the whole floor – this amount will depend on how thick texture is to be. If in doubt about how much to mix up, it is better to under-estimate and mix up more later, rather than mix up too much and have loads left over. As with all paints, there will be a guide as to the coverage on all brands. Then, having protected the surroundings with plenty of polythene, start spraying. Unlike the sophisticated design of a gravity feed-gun, in spray painting (*see* Chapter 14) a spray texture gun is a very basic design. The moment the compressor is switched on, texture will start to be pushed through the nozzle, even before the trigger is pulled: so treat it with care. Spraying on the floor is quite straightforward, but be extra careful when working on upright scenery, as it can be tempting to hold the gun above shoulder level and risk coverage of yourself as the texture tips out.

The effect of these guns is adjustable from a finer speckled texture to a far coarser effect. A method of smoothing out certain areas with a wet trowel is highly effective also.

Creating Brickwork

To make a highly effective and relatively inexpensive effect here, first mark out all the bricks, choosing a type such as London stock. To help in drawing these out, it is advisable to mark out the divisions on a long piece of stick, and use ½in masking tape for the mortar, leaving a little overhang at the edges. Once all the mortar has been masked out, leaving the bricks clear, start spraying. The only really important thing to remember here, is that all the tape must be removed before the texture has dried, otherwise it is very difficult to remove. When these are painted, the difference in texture between bricks and mortar help to define them, and they look great. This technique is particularly good for productions with a small budget, which cannot afford vacforms.

Brickwork created by texture gun and masking tape.

Bricks used for the RADA production of Birds on the Wing, *designed by Matthew Wright and directed by Guy Slater.*

PRE-MOULDED TEXTURES

As explained earlier, the invention of vacforming and pre-moulds was highly beneficial to scenic art and design. However, like most things in life, they have their disadvantages as well as their advantages. The main disadvantage to many amateur or smaller venues is the cost, as it is relatively expensive. The other is that, over a large expanse, it is difficult to disguise certain repetitive patterns such as brickwork. The advantages are that it is extremely lightweight, which is ideal for touring companies. Also, a vacform mould can be made out of most objects, such as architectural mouldings, pebbles, wall surfaces, bottles, bark, etc.

How to Affix Pre-Moulded Textures

For affixing vacform to a fabric surface, such as a canvassed flat, it is wiser to use a contact adhesive (following the appropriate health and safety measures), and back this up with the use of staples around the wood edges. If trying to disguise the fact that there are edges and

177

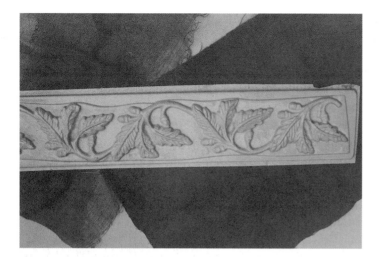

An example of vacform.

repeats, such as for brickwork, it is a good idea to trim all the edges and then cut out certain bricks in an irregular manner, so that the next one will fit like a piece of jigsaw to it. The same process goes for affixing to wooden flattage. It is a good idea to continue the staples irregularly across the whole piece, as it tends to sag once the scenery is erected, destroying the illusion completely.

Preparation and Priming

Before painting vacform you will need to coat it with a layer of specialist prime, available from specialist retailers, before any emulsion, acrylic or textures can be applied. This prime can also be tinted with colour if required, prior to any subsequent processes.

CARVING AND APPLIED TEXTURES

The final category of scenic textures to take a look at is basic carving and texturing of polystyrene, and the application of textures such as sponge or foam. Using these techniques can create some highly effective results, which can look particularly stunning under lighting.

Basic Carving

The overall term for any material such as polystyrene is a foamed plastic, and there are many brands and types that come under this heading. To simplify in a basic description such as this, the material polystyrene will be used as an example. As it is a synthetic material, it is also highly flammable, and must be scrimmed or painted with a highly effective fire-retarder before being used on stage – this is very important.

As polystyrene is such a flexible material, it is very pliable to work with, unlike stone or wood. This can be a disadvantage; caution is required at first, until confidence is gained of its nature. The advantage for theatre is that it is so lightweight. Depending on the effect required from the polystyrene, a variety of tools can be used such as knives, sand-paper, wire brushes or any personal invention.

An Example of Basic Polystyrene Carving
Using your design reference, work out the scale in the method described in Chapter 12. First, draw out the image on to the surface: this can be done either directly on to the polystyrene, or by using a stencil and spraying the design on to the surface. A stencil can be particularly useful when there is much repetition of letters,

patterns or numbers. Using a sharp knife, cut out the images, taking care not to cut out too much, as it will not be possible to replace it! (A word of warning: never do any cutting pointing the blade towards yourself, only ever away from your body.) A bit of wire-brushing and sand-papering across the finished piece will enhance the textural surface. Finally, this needs to be protected, either by a specialist coating, available through scenic stockists, or by scrimming. Either will give a really good protective surface, as well as creating a lovely surface to start painting on.

An example of basic scenic carving tools, and an effective example of polystyrene carving that works really well under stage lighting.

APPLIED TEXTURES

An excellent example to illustrate this category are the hedges created for a production of *A Clandestine Marriage* at RADA. Here the designer required a heavily textured look for the topiary hedges, which play an integral role in the plot of the play, and it was important that they looked solid and believable. The budget did not allow for any pre-made prop privet, and time and budget did not allow for any carving. It was, therefore, decided to use foam off-cuts that were glued on to the fine metal mesh surfaces with a fire-retardant contact adhesive. This was then texture gun-sprayed with a mix of Idenden, which added a fire-protective coating, as well as adding to the overall effect. This

An example of applied textures on the set for A Clandestine Marriage. *Chipped foam spray textured with Idenden formed a highly textural and striking effect.*

Scrimming

Scrimming is a scenic process used for the protection of materials such as polystyrene, and as a fire-retarder. Depending on the scale and complexity of design, slightly overlapping small or larger cut pieces of scenic muslin are glued over the entire piece allowing for no gaps. The mix of glue was historically made of a glue size, but can now be done in a watered down PVA mix. Allowing for slight shrinkage, the pieces must each be put into place with the aid of short stamping movements, using an old short-bristled brush, so that the muslin follows the contours of the design. Once this has dried, it is a fantastic hard and protected surface.

was an economical, quick and highly effective process that looked very convincing under lighting – so much so that an elderly lady of the audience was seen to pick off a piece in the interval!

As shown by these descriptions, there are many ways of creating a texture. For applied textures, a variety of other materials can be used, all depending on the effect required. It will often be the scenic artist's job to come up with an inspired idea. These could include:

* fabrics, such as muslins, hessians, underfelts, carpet and jute scrim, which can be applied scrunched up or stretched to give variations;
* natural materials, such as cork, sand or sawdust which, instead of being added to a wet mixture, can be sprinkled over a glued surface to create a texture on their own, for example fine sawdust sprinkled over a glued surface can resemble a fine suede wall-covering, and is far cheaper.

16 THREE-DIMENSIONAL TEXTURING AND EFFECTS

This chapter will cover the use of materials to create natural and architectural features, as well as the use of mouldings in the construction of cornice work using layered rather than solid materials. The materials will largely consist of those that are readily available from builders' merchants, rather than self-generated materials. This chapter will be tied together through the construction and finishing of a variety of specific set pieces.

Why do we work in the theatre? Clearly it is not for the sociable hours or possibility of retiring wealthy by the age of forty! With little chance of permanent employment in an industry that is influenced more than most by the whims of an unpredictable public, it is safe to say that there must be something else to attract us. Ask virtually anyone connected with the industry and they will give the same answer: variety of work. This chapter highlights this point very clearly. Although a certain amount of time is spent doing the more mundane

matters, such as flat building or priming, often greater challenges arise to test both the scenic carpenter and artist.

CHALLENGE ONE: TO CREATE A REALISTIC CORNICE FOR THE TOP OF A GEORGIAN-PERIOD DOOR FLAT

Many sets require similar items and it is impossible, for a variety of reasons, to use a real cornice. Either the cost or the weight of an actual plaster cornice would prove prohibitive to use and, if a vacuum-former is not available, the carpenter has a real problem. However, with a quick visit to a builder's merchants, it is a far from insurmountable one. Let us look at how to solve this specific challenge.

As a rule, the designer will have provided a guideline to the size they require of the cornice itself. Using 18mm ply, form a right-angle

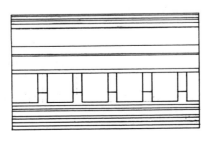 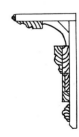

Front and side elevation of wooden composite cornice construction.

channel to these dimensions and then build the cornice using this as the base.

A simple trick is to incorporate quarter-round polystyrene coving to the inside corner of the channel, sticking it in position using contact adhesive. This creates a pleasing curve to the inner part of the cornice with the added weight advantage.

Along the bottom edge of the coving, run a length of 25 × 75mm PAR softwood on flat with a length of 19 × 50mm torus architrave planted on the bottom edge. Along the top edge of the cornice, simply run another length of the 19 × 50mm torus architrave. Next, cut a number of blocks 75mm long from some 25 × 75mm PAR softwood. Fix these vertically along the bottom edge with 20mm spacings in between each one. Cut a number of blocks 20mm long from 12 × 20mm PAR softwood and glue these in between each of the vertical blocks. Finally, add a length of 25 × 50mm astragal moulding to the bottom edge and a length of 12 × 19mm astragal to edge of the top piece of 18mm ply.

The beauty of this method is that it is completely self-supporting and can be applied effectively to touring, as well as repertory, sets. An 18mm structure can be easily fixed to the set and they are reasonably heavy, so care should be taken to ensure adequate support to the flattage during and after installation.

CHALLENGE TWO: TO CREATE A CRUCIFIX THAT WILL WITHSTAND THE WEIGHT OF AN ACTOR

A crucifix or cross is something that has a habit of appearing in a variety of productions, varying from well-known musicals to passion plays. It would be a simple matter to construct a cross out of solid timber, however one attempt to lift it would prove detrimental to the actor's back.

As well as this, the cost of solid timber would prove prohibitive. To solve both of these problems, a simple box construction will suffice – but what about nails? It is somewhat traditional to hammer nails into the horizontal member of the cross and, unless a light hollow noise is required, some modification is necessary.

It is suggested that to create a substantial enough looking construction, a box section of 150 × 150mm should be aimed for.

In addition to the above dimensions, the technical drawing shows some other useful information. The position of the footstep is vital, as this should be glued and screwed through from behind prior to construction of the box. Also, note that the areas where the hands will be positioned on the cross member have been filled with solid timber. This will allow for repeated hammering over a season of crucifixions!

The construction of the crucifix itself is a straightforward one, with a series of butt joints incorporated to create a lightweight cross. Fix all the elements together using nails and glue. Use a nail punch to drive the head well into the timber in preparation for distressing – this term refers to the process of making newly dressed timber appear aged.

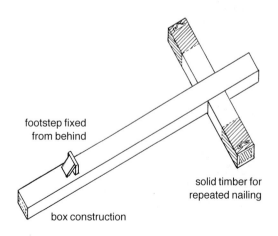

footstep fixed from behind

solid timber for repeated nailing

box construction

Crucifix construction.

Timber Distressing

Timber distressing tools include:

* hatchet
* chains
* disc-sander
* blowtorch
* sand-blaster.

The most useful distressing tool is the hatchet, which can be used to take substantial amounts of timber off corners in an extremely fast manner. It is a quick, cheap and an easy tool to use,

Health and Safety

Start slowly, taking a little off at a time and always remember that the cross is held together with nails. It takes much less time to drive the nails further into the timber with a nail punch than it does to re-grind the hatchet. Make sure that the timber that you are working on is securely fixed to the work surface, naturally health and safety is paramount in this situation, and eye and hand protection must be used.

Set photo from **Son of Man,** *RADA, designed by Julie Nelson and directed by Robin Midgely, showing distressed timber.*

with the added advantage of creating enormous biceps for the user! In the case of the present challenge, the hatchet will give an excellent effect to all the corners of the cross.

Using a disc-sander will distress the face of the timber in the same way as the hatchet affects the edges. Timber today is supplied with an immaculate surface, however, this has not always been the case. The disc-sander breaks the smooth planes of dressed timber very effectively creating a hand-hewn effect. Remember to wear gloves, as well as eye and ear protection, when using a disc-sander – although it appears to be a reasonably innocuous tool, it is capable of giving a nasty graze.

The last tool that will be used for this project is the chain. Wearing strong leather gloves and eye protection, hit the timber with a length of 20mm-link chain. This will create the effect of the cross having had a life before the play began. It will look like it has been knocked against obstacles and generally will appear more worn than new timber.

The last two distressing tools are not required for this challenge, however they are used regularly in all sorts of set construction. The blow-torch can scorch timber, giving a textural as well as ageing effect, whilst the sand-blaster can be used to remove the soft timber from the grain leaving the hard, raised sections of the grain. This can be particularly effective when used on flooring to give a highly contrasting finish.

With the cross completed, it is ready for painting and finishing, and is handed over to the scenic department to complete the job! It is decided that, in order to accentuate the existing distressed effect, an additional textured graining would be added before the cross is painted. This is done using a mixture of tinted Idenden, and a comb and grainer is used to create a distinctive raised grain. When dried, the cross is painted using a mixture of wet and dry brushing techniques in order to make the most of the textures on the wood.

CHALLENGE THREE: CREATE A DESERT FLOOR WITHOUT THE USE OF SAND

In this show, a floor surface is required that would simulate a dry and dusty floor surface for the play *Son of Man* by Dennis Potter. Both time and the budget are limited, which subsequently rules out the use of any expensive or time-consuming scenic techniques, such as carved polystyrene, fibreglassing or gesmonite textures. The audience seats are incorporated into the design and placed directly onto the floor, which extends to the outer edges of the entire studio theatre. A few problems have to be taken into careful consideration.

* Any texturing on a floor has to be particularly resilient in order to withstand the action of the actors, technical staff during fit-up period and, in this case, the audience as well, for a period of ten shows.
* The budget is limited, and where Idenden may have done the trick in terms of strength and flexibility, it is simply far too costly in terms of the amount needed to cover the entire floor.
* As part of the play, the crucifix has to be dragged across an area of the stage, which means that the surface cannot afford to be so impenetrable so as to not create any marks at all.

It is decided, after some careful sampling, and gaining the approval of the designer, that a mixture of Artex, a powder-form textured finish, and PVA will be used. Initial sampling shows that when the texture is applied to a hardboard surface by means of a texture gun, it lifts straight off when it has dried, without much persuasion. However, when it is sprayed onto a hardboard surface covered in jute scrim, not only does it stick but creates some great natural organic shapes as well, which closely

The final effect of the **Son of Man** *floor, which comes alive under lighting. A RADA production, designed by Julie Nelson and directed by Robin Midgely.*

resemble the original references given by the designer.

The processes then are as follows: the entire floor is covered in jute scrim, stuck down with rollers using building PVA thinned with water. This then creates the perfect surface for the Artex to be texture sprayed onto.

Many buckets are mixed up, each with an extra addition of PVA, and the entire area surrounding the floor is masked off prior to the big spray. Certain areas are treated to greater amounts of spray than others, in an attempt to simulate subtle undulations of the desert floor. The vital thing that is needed is time, in order for the whole floor to dry, as well as double-checking that all hardboards are firmly affixed to the actu-

al floor, as a great deal of moisture is to sit there for a couple of days until dry.

When the floor has dried and natural cracks and undulations have appeared over the drying process, the final effect is strong, resilient and remarkably desert like. Once painted in the dusty pinks and pale ochres of sand, areas are rubbed down with pieces of old gauze, which helps to reveal the natural whiteness of the Artex, and the only process left to do, is to seal the entire area with an excellent quality water-based floor sealent. The price for the entire floor comes to well within the given budget.

These three challenges are typical of those faced by both scenic carpenter and artist. In a profession where a large budget is not very often available, there may well be situations like these where using practical resourcefulness is an integral part of the job description and, what is more, it can be more satisfying than one might imagine!

CONCLUSION

The completion of a set, making those final touch-ups and minor alterations required before the opening night, bring about a sense of achievement for all of those involved. This is where all of those who have taken part in the set construction and scenic art processes take a step backwards as the performers step forward on the stage and the show begins its run. A small amount of work may be required in maintaining a set but, more often than not, we are in the process of thinking about our next venture, whether employed on a full-time basis or as a freelancer. We can be confident in the knowledge that, yet again, a new set will bring about as many surprises and new experiences as the last. This element of anticipation is arguably a choice for those of us in life who enjoy a regular challenge in our chosen careers.

The reader will have become aware that there is certainly more to a stage set than initially meets the eye, and the range of skills required in order to work as a scenic carpenter or artist is diverse. A training in either of these crafts, either through college or an apprenticeship, will undoubtedly prepare the individual for a career, which, if so required, extends further than the theatre and on into interior design and other entertainment fields.

Be prepared for many long and unsocial hours, but confident in the fact that it can be a highly fulfilling and really enjoyable job, where the phrase 'living to work' is more attributable than 'working to live'.

FURTHER READING

Anatomy

Muybridge, E., *The Male and Female Figure in Motion* (Dover Publications, 1984)

Schider, F., *An Atlas of Anatomy for Artists* (Dover Publications, 1957)

Architecture

Fletcher, Sir B., *The History of Architecture* (Academic Press/Butterworth Heinemann, 1996)

Morris, H. M. (trans.) Vitruvius *The Ten Books on Architecture* (Dover Publications, 1960)

Illustrated Dictionary of Historic Architecture. Edited by Cyril M Harris (Dover Publications, 1977)

Colour, Materials and Techniques

Delamare, G., *Colour: Making and Using Dyes and Pigments* (Thames and Hudson, 2000)

Itten, J., *The Art of Colour* (Reinhold Publishing Corporation, 1961)

Jarman, D., *Chroma* (Vintage, 1995)

Mayer, R., *The Artist's Handbook of Materials and Techniques* (Viking Press, 1940)

Decorative Art

Sales Meyer, F., *Handbook of Ornament* (Dover Publications, 1957)

Speltz, A., *The Styles of Ornament* (Dover Publications, 1959)

General Interest

Harwood, R., *All the World's A Stage* (Methuen, 1984)

Lucie-Smith, E., *Dictionary of Art Terms* (Thames and Hudson, 1984)

Blossfeldt, K., *Art Forms in the Plant World* (Dover Publications, 1986)

Perspective

Cole, R. V., *Perspective for the Artist* (Dover Publications, 1976)

Specialist: Scenic Art and Design

Crabtree, Susan, and Beudert, Peter, *Scenic Art for the Theatre: History, Tools and Techniques* (Focal Press, 1998)

Craig, E. G., *On the Art of Theatre* (Theatre Arts Books, 1957)

Goodwin, J. (ed.) *British Theatre Design. The Modern Age* (Weidenfeld & Nicholson, 1989)

Hoggett, C., *Stage Crafts* (A & C Black, 1975)

Pecktal, L., *Designing and Painting for the Theatre* (Holt, Rinehart and Winston, 1975)

Polunin, V., *The Continental Method of Scene Painting* (Dance Books Ltd, 1927)

Reid, F., *The Staging Handbook* (A & C Black, 1978)

Thorne, G., *Theatre Design: a Practical Guide* (The Crowood Press, 1999)

Textures

Brodatz, P., *Textures, a Photographic Album for Artists and Designers* (Dover Publications, 1966)

Juracek, J. A., *Surfaces* (Thames and Hudson, 1996)

Wood-Graining and Marbling

Rhodes, B., and Windsor, J., *Parry's Graining and Marbling* (BSP Professional Books, 1949)

Useful Addresses

Flint Hire and Supply Ltd: theatrical chandlers.
Queens Row, London SE17 2PX.
Tel: 020 7703 9786. Fax: 020 7708 4189.
  Email: sales@flints.co.uk. www.flints.co.uk

Brian Josephs Hardware Company: theatrical
  suppliers.
Scenery House, 2 Hereward Road, London
  SW17 7EY.
Tel: 020 8767 2887. Fax: 020 8767 0849.

The Clow Group Ltd: Heffers brushes, and
  general painting equipment.
562–584 Lea Bridge Road, Leyton, London
  E10 7DW.
Tel: 020 8558 0300. Fax: 020 8558 0301.

Artists Materials
Russell and Chapple: scenic canvas suppliers.
68 Drury Lane, London WC2B 5SP.
Tel: 020 7836 7521.
  Email:info@randc.net

L. Cornelissen & Son Ltd.
105 Great Russell Street, London WC1B 3RY.
Tel: 020 7636 1045. Fax: 020 7636 3655.
  Email: info@cornelissen.com

Decorative and Specialist Paints
J. W. Bollom and Co Ltd.
Croydon Road, Beckenham, Kent BR3 4BL.
Tel: 020 8658 2299. Fax: 020 8658 8672.
  www.bollom.com

John Myland Ltd.
80 Norwood High Street, West Norwood,
  London SE27 9NW.
Tel: 020 8670 9161. Fax: 020 8761 5700.
  Email: sales@mylands.co.uk
  www.mylands.co.uk

Bristol UK Ltd.
12 The Arches, Maygrove Road, London
  NW6 2DS.
Tel: 020 7624 0686. Fax: 020 7372 5242.
  www.bristolpaint.com

Roscolab Ltd.
Blanchard Works, Kangley Bridge Road,
  Sydenham SE26 5AQ.
Tel: 020 8659 2300. Fax: 020 8659 3153.
  Email: marketing@roscolab.co.uk
  www.rosco.com

Brodie and Middleton Ltd.
68 Drury Lane, London WC2B 5SP.
Tel: 020 7836 3289. Fax: 020 7497 0554.
  Email: info@randc.net

Health and Safety
HSE: Health and Safety Executive.
Information Centre, Broad Lane, Sheffield
  S3 7HQ.

HSE Books.
PO Box 1999, Sudbury, Suffolk CO10 2WA.
Tel: 01787 881165. Fax: 01787 313995.

HSE Home page: www.open.gov.uk/hse/
  hsehome.htm
Info line: 0541 545500.

ROSPA (Royal Society for the Prevention of
  Accidents)
Edgbaston Park, 353 Bristol Road,
  Birmingham B5 7ST.
Tel: 0121 248 2000.
  www.rospa.co.uk

Specialist Books
French's Theatre Bookshop.
52 Fitzroy Street, London W1T 5JR.
Tel: 020 7387 9373. Fax: 020 7387 2161.
  Email: theatre@samualfrench.co.uk

The Dover Bookshop.
18 Earlham Street, London WC2H 9LG.
Tel: 020 7836 2111. Fax: 020 7836 1603.
  Email: images@thedoverbookshop.com
  www.doverbooks.co.uk

Dance Books Ltd.
The Old Bakery, 4 Lenten Street, Alton,
  Hants.
Tel: 01420 86142. Fax: 01420 86142.
  Email: dl@dancebooks.co.uk
  www.dancebooks.co.uk

Spray-Gun Manufacturers
Devilbiss.Ransburg.Binks
ITW Finishing UK.
Ringwood Road, Bournemouth BH11 9LH

Stage Drapes, Scenery and Drapery Fabrics
J. D. McDougall Ltd.
4 McGrath Road, London E15 4JP.
Tel: 020 8534 2921. Fax: 020 8519 8423.
  Email: sales@mcdougall.co.uk

Gerriets Great Britain Ltd.
18 Verney Road, London SE16 3DH.
Tel: 020 7639 7704. Fax: 020 7732 5760.
  Email: gerriets_gb@compuserve.com

Prompt Side Ltd.
Theatrical Drapery, 3 British Wharf,
  Landmann Way, London SE14 5RS.
Tel: 020 8694 8164. Fax: 020 8694 8169.
  www.promptside.co.uk

Ken Creasey Ltd.
Theatrical Suppliers, 34 Queens Row, London
  SE17 2PX.
Tel: 020 7277 1645. Fax: 020 7277 1701.

J. C Joel Ltd: theatrical drapes and stage
  manufacturers.
Corporation Mill, Corporation Street, Sowerby
  Bridge, Halifax HX6 2QQ.
Tel: 01422 833 835. Fax: 01422 835 157.
  Email: mail@joel.demon.co.uk
  www.jcjoel.co.uk

Timber Suppliers
Arnold Laver Timber World
Head Office, Bramall Lane, Sheffield S2 4RJ.
Tel: 0114 255 6161. Fax: 0114 250 9387.

Reading Branch, Basingstoke Road, Reading
  RG2 0QN.
Tel: 0118 930 4777. Fax: 0118 930 4888.

INDEX